S	A	T	O	R
A	R	E	P	O
T	E	N	E	T
O	P	E	R	A
R	O	T	A	S

The Powwow Grimoire

ISBN 9781501096822

The reader assumes all responsibility for any and all attempts made to utilize the charms and cures found within this work. The use of cultural-specific folk magic is a subject that is understood by few, accepted by even less, and workable by even less than that. Proceed at your own risk. Always seek proper medical attention when necessary and encourage others to do the same.

3rd Edition 2017

2nd Edition 2015

1st Edition 2014 under the author name Robert Matthew Chapman

The Powwow Grimoire

Robert Phoenix

Being a compendium of knowledge and lore for the practitioner of

Pennsylvania German Powwow.

Lemoyne, Pennsylvania

Cumberland County

Third Edition, 2017

Whosoever possesses this book shall be protected by

Almighty God.

In the name of the Father, Son, and Holy Ghost.

+ + +

This work is dedicated to Bill and Josani, the family that God has blessed me with. I also dedicate this work to our loving fur and fin babies; Chip, Harry, Arthur, Danny, Pink Fish, and, forever my best friend, Frodo.

Forward

In 2014, when I first put together this book, I had no idea it would become as popular as it did. I was very pleased to learn that so many people were interested in the subject of Pennsylvania German Powwowing. I was even more pleased that they enjoyed and benefited from my work. Over the past few years I have been adding to my experiences as a practitioner of Powwow and so I felt it was time to give this book a facelift and some much-needed updates. Some formatting changes were made, some editing to various bits of text have been made, and a few other changes and adjustments were made that I felt would add to the overall look and flow of the book. While the content from the original edition is largely still here, you will notice that the arrangement of the information is completely different. There were various reasons for this, many of which you probably won't care about, so I'll just say that this new and improved edition should satisfy those who had issues with the original.

As always, I hope you enjoy and learn from what you read in these pages. I am by no means the ultimate authority on the subject of Powwowing, but this book represents my voice within the tradition. It is my wish that my input remains a part of the ongoing conversation amongst practitioners, and someday I hope to read your thoughts on the subject.

May God bless you always.

Robert Phoenix

October 22, 2017

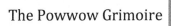

Table of Contents

Introduction

For over 200 years, the tradition of Pennsylvania German Powwowing has enjoyed continuous adherence amongst the Pennsylvania German community. As a practitioner of the tradition, I feel it is the responsible thing for me to put forth proper information in regards to the practice of Powwowing so that its future is assured. Powwowing is a part of the culture of the Pennsylvania Germans and, as such, should be respected in its cultural, historical, and traditional contexts. This work, as with all of my work in regards to Powwow, is a testament to my love and respect for the culture from which it comes.

By what authority does one call himself a practitioner of the tradition? I would answer this question with a question of my own: *Why do you want to become a practitioner?* Your reasons for choosing to learn how to Powwow become the foundation of your practice and the force which drives you to help those in need who come to you for healing, protection, curse removals, and the like.

The work of a Powwow is not glamorous. It will not make you famous. It will not make you wealthy. Indeed, your work will go largely unnoticed outside of your immediate community. But it's still important work.

What is the work of a Powwow? A Powwow is a healer, first and foremost. He is a healer that uses his God-given abilities to serve his community. Much like the Cunning Men of England, a Powwow is also a remover of curses, known here in Pennsylvania German culture as *hexerei. Hexerei* is the practice of malevolent witchcraft. The word *hex* is the German word for witch. The work of a Powwow includes the removal of *hexerei* cast upon individuals, family lines, households, farms, and so forth. This is an important element to consider because, also like the Cunning Men of England (which has many of the same roots and practices as Powwow), the practice of anti-*hexerei* work is an essential piece of the tradition. Pennsylvania has a long and complex history of *hexerei* and the Powwow has always been there to combat it. In addition to healing

The Powwow Grimoire

S	A	T	O	R
A	R	E	P	O
T	E	N	E	T
O	P	E	R	A
R	O	T	A	S

and curse removal, the Powwow may also help with other household or farm issues, such as sick horses or cows, blighted crops, and the like. And finally, to be a Powwow is to feel called to do so.

It's important for me to mention that there are different methods by which one claims the title of Powwow, as has always been the case throughout the history of the tradition. You will find that this is true within almost any magical tradition. There are some who believe that Powwowing can only be passed from male to female and so on, in an unbroken lineage. This was a common means of transmission of the tradition throughout history, although not the exclusive method by which individuals became practitioners. Some sources show that it was common for Powwowing to be taught from father to son or mother to daughter; passing on the ability through same-gender lines within the family. There are some who shun this same-gender method and insist only on cross-gender teaching. To these individuals I would only say that while I have great respect for this idea, and respect your adherence to it, the sheer number of practitioners throughout our state's history does not support this exclusive claim. Therefore, with respect to the lineaged practitioners, I would ask *"Who trained the first Powwow?"* Indeed, the vast majority of practitioners that have been interviewed over the past two hundred years for medical journals, newspaper articles, and the like, work with charms and cures as found within the most well-known Grimoire written on the tradition of Powwowing: *The Long Lost Friend* (or any of its later variants). It's important to note that *The Long Lost Friend* (later renamed "Powwows", hence the name of the tradition) bears no mention of transmission through cross-gender or same-gender teachings. In fact, the work assumes that the reader will be using the information found within, with absolutely no indication that this is improper. As you are reading through my work, you may assume that I feel the same.

Another influential source of Powwow material (and indeed, much of *The Long Lost Friend* was copied from this work) is the book *Egyptian Secrets of Albertus Magnus*. In the Introduction, the reader receives this message, *"But to him who properly esteems and values this book, and never abuses its teachings, will not only be granted the usefulness of its contents, but he will also attain everlasting joy and blessing…"* In other words, it was written with the purpose of using the material found within. There is no mention of having to be taught or initiated by a member of the opposite sex (or the same sex, for that matter).

I personally have received what is known as "lineaged" instruction (taught by a woman who learned from a man) but those teachings are not going to be found within these pages out of respect for the lady who taught me. She asked me to not share her name, likely for fear that she would find herself bombarded with requests for healing or teaching, and I have respected her request for many years.

There is also a curious method, often mentioned in older articles on the subject of Powwowing whereby one can learn by means of eavesdropping on a practitioner while he is teaching an inanimate object, such as a chair or table. This silly method supposedly bypasses the cross-gender limitation that some impose. While there are many practitioners over the past two hundred years that have mentioned this method of learning, I have never come across anyone who claims to have learned in this manner.

There are others, like myself, who have blood ties to the culture of the Pennsylvania Germans and, as such, choose to practice Powwowing because it is a tradition rooted in our own culture. One thing that must be understood here is that Pennsylvania Germans are not exclusively from Germany, although a vast majority of them were. Rather, our ancestry hails from Switzerland, Bohemia, Moravia, Austria, France, and of course Germany. They were *German-speaking* immigrants that later blended with the English that were already here in Pennsylvania and this blending created a unique culture that became known as Pennsylvania German (or Pennsylvania Dutch, as the locals call it). Just because one has German ancestry, does not mean one has Pennsylvania German ancestry, and the opposite is also true.

Still, there are other Powwowers who, having inclinations to the mystical and mysterious, and being proper and good Christians, chose to blend these aspects of their lives and take up the practice of Powwowing. The Gospels do provide us with some precedent:

Mark 16:15-18

He said to them, "Go into all the world and preach the gospel to all creation. Whoever believes and is baptized will be saved, but whoever does not believe will be condemned. And these signs will accompany those who believe: In my name they will drive out demons; they will speak in new tongues; they will pick up snakes with their hands; and when they drink deadly poison, it will not hurt them at all; they will place their hands on sick people, and they will get well."

And so the crux of this work is a tradition rooted in Christian faith, ancestral culture, Pennsylvania pride, local history, folklore, and magic. Powwow can be little understood outside of any of these influences, which is why it has such a small following and has barely traveled outside of the state of Pennsylvania. Indeed, there are Germans in the western part of Pennsylvania that have never even heard of Powwowing. Refer to my earlier statement of German vs. Pennsylvania German for an explanation of this.

What follows is the tradition of Powwowing as it is understood in its most wide scope. For most, Powwowing involves nothing more than simple cures for common ailments; such as scrapes, burns, and the like. For others, Powwowing encompasses not only the folk remedies of the common people but also the ceremonial "high magic" of the more occult-oriented. These elements are a nod to Powwow's roots in the old Grimoire traditions; much of which has influenced other modern magical traditions and lodges, but discussion of those is beyond the scope of this work.

The purpose of this work is to present the wide array of practices that are, or can be, found within the tradition known as Powwow.

My claim to this tradition is on several levels. On one hand, my family has Pennsylvania German lines which are traced to Austria. In the mid 1800's, my Great Great Grandfather and Grandmother came to Pennsylvania from Stiermark, Austria in search of a new life and religious freedom. They were members of the German Reformed Church but in Austria the Catholic Church ruled, so they fled and followed William Penn's promise of a haven of religious freedom. Because the German-speaking immigrants kept such close-knit communities, by the time my siblings and I were born, our family was deeply immersed in the Pennsylvania German culture. I grew up with the foods, décor, environment, and ideals of the Pennsylvania German culture. My grandfather was the last in our family to speak Pennsylvania German so the dialect was sadly lost within my family. From the Great-greats who immigrated here in the mid 1800's all the way down to me, the paternal side of my family has maintained membership in the Reformed Church, which in more recent times merged with the Lutheran Church to become known as a Union Church. In even more recent times, the Union Church reformed to become The United Church of Christ. My adherence to the religious traditions of my ancestors is a testament to my respect for family tradition. My adherence to Powwowing is a testament to my love for the culture and folklore of my family.

Another claim I make to the tradition is its development in the state I live in. I was born and raised in Pennsylvania and firmly believe that we are most in tune with the magic and religions not only of our ancestry, but also of the land from which we come. It seems to be a product of modern thinking that magic from lands far away in time and space and romanticized to the point of fantastical are the most interesting. However, I have found that the land I'm from has power of its own. Powwowing was born and developed in the area of the world I am from therefore I claim it as my right by locale and birth.

I do have a lineaged connection to the tradition, having been taught two charms in the traditional cross-gender method. But, as mentioned earlier, those charms will not be found within any of my published works on the tradition out of respect to the lady who taught me.

Finally, I make claim to the tradition of Powwowing by virtue of Jesus Christ and the calling I experienced to follow Him and become a Powwow during a particularly dark period of my life. I will not trouble you with the specifics, but let's just say that God intervened in my life and set me on the path to where I am today. I have been following this path with a more strict adherence to tradition ever since. Any additions I have made to my practice of Powwow that are considered to be outside the normal parameters for the tradition (such as with some of the ceremonial pieces), have been done so carefully so as to maintain the cultural, historical, and religious truths of Powwowing.

Powwowing is, by its very nature, a Christian practice. Any other interpretation is completely modern and unknown within Pennsylvania German culture and therefore intentionally left out of this work.

What follows is my interpretation of the Powwowing tradition based on history, academia, culture, fact, religious affiliation, and verifiable evidence. It is no easy task to trace the history of a complex tradition such as Powwowing, and indeed that historical information is largely beyond the scope of this work. Please visit my website www.PAGermanPowwow.com for more historical information.

What the reader of this work can expect to find is the most comprehensive collection of charms, cures, and ritualistic elements that I could piece together over the years. Some of this is largely unknown to the common folk practitioner of Powwowing. However, to the more ceremonially-inclined, this work represents the deeper elements that are often referred to as "High Magic". All of this work comes from historically and culturally appropriate sources. All can be found by research on your own, and nothing contained herein is a product of secret or lineaged teachings. I have attempted to preserve the work as I learned it through study, practice, and the assistance of others schooled in the tradition and culture.

As a nearly final note in this rather lengthy introduction, I will say that I do not speak the Pennsylvania German language. There are some who believe the charms are ineffective if spoken in English. I have not found this to be true at all. Therefore, everything provided to you within this Grimoire is in English. Should you desire the original German for many of the charms, you can easily find this information through further research and study on your own.

And lastly, know that the charms, cures, and rituals found herein assume a Christian worldview, as they have always. There is no evidence to suggest that Powwowing was ever anything but

Christian. And certainly there is nothing (other than the word "powwow") to suggest that there are any connections to Native American spirituality, despite erroneous claims to the contrary. Therefore, I wrap up this piece of the Grimoire with words which come to us from another well-known Powwowing Grimoire, *The Sixth and Seventh Books of Moses*:

"One thing must not be omitted, in conclusion, and that is, we must first become Christians before we can perform cures by Christian methods. Very few are really Christians who call themselves such; they are only Christians in name and appearance. The art of healing, according to scriptural principles, deserves special mention in this place, in more than one respect, not only because something truly magical takes place therein, but because scriptural healing is often regarded as the only true one. The principles of this art of healing have been fully established according to certain declarations and doctrines of the Bible."

Chapter One

The Powwow Doctor

Whether you make the conscious decision to learn some Powwowing charms or you feel it is a calling from God, or maybe someone in your family decided to teach you a charm or two that they know, you'll find that being a Powwow is life changing in some ways.

For starters, it gives you a more active role in your religion. I believe this is why folk magic is so prevalent throughout many cultures, both in modern times and in the past. The practice of folk magic alongside your own homespun version of your religion, which is known as "folk religion", is a means of helping people feel they are a part of their religious beliefs, rather than a mere spectator in a show every Sunday morning. Folk religion, and by extension folk magic, are empowering because they provide evidence of something greater than ourselves and give us a part to play in bringing the healing power of our God into the world. I realize that may sound slightly dramatic, but there you go.

Another important life change that occurred with me (and may be true for you as well) was that Powwowing taught me what my own limits are and so therefore took pressure away from me to impress others with what I was doing. In the beginning, I wanted to be amazing with my Powwowing. I wanted to be known as a great healer and a faithful believer in my religion. Over time, however, the pressure I was putting on myself was really weighing me down. The fact is, sometimes the healing charms don't work. And when that happened, I was blaming myself. But I eventually learned that this was the wrong way to experience Powwowing. Once I learned to let go of all that pressure and accept that I will not always be the right choice for some people, I was able to have more positive experiences and successes with my work and eliminate all of that pressure to have others approve of me. If you are seeking approval or fame or some sort of notoriety with your Powwowing, I'm sorry to say that you will be disappointed.

The Powwow Doctor is a Christian. But unlike some other magical traditions, Powwowing is neither flashy nor showy nor does it require the use of costumes or props. There is no need for candles or incense or soft new age harp music. There are no group meetings of Powwowers or ritualistic ceremonies to celebrate holy days other than what you'll experience at your own church.

The Powwow tradition is simplistic to the point of not seeming like a tradition at all. It fits nicely into your already established religion as it comes from Biblical sources. You can learn a few charms and use them as the situations present themselves. And that's pretty much it.

You will not need to alter your personality or wardrobe in any fashion and certainly you won't need to go out and purchase anything in order to make your Powwowing more successful. There are no altars to set up or chambers of magic to build onto your home. At most you'll want to have a straight hard-back chair handy so your client can sit down. Keep your Bible close by. And other than some string, a smooth stone, and a small knife (a pocket knife is fine, and if it has a red handle that's even better), that's pretty much it.

Later on we will discuss further ceremonial techniques that you can certainly add to your private work, should you desire to bring an extra religious element into your Powwowing. This would be entirely optional on your part. I first incorporated the ceremonial elements into my own work because I had a desire to have a ritualistic experience and I just didn't feel that I was getting satisfied in this way at my church. So it was a means for me to have a more active religious experience on my own. You may choose to do the same as me or you may never find interest in the more ceremonial possibilities. And that's ok. It doesn't make you more or less of a Powwow.

Some magical traditions may dictate certain clothing or ritual items to wear when practicing magic. Powwow is not like this. I have read in a few places that a Powwower must wear a hat. I personally do not see the necessity of this. However, there are a few charms (mostly anti-hex work) that require you to use your hat.

So for these charms, I would say a hat might be necessary. It is not necessary that you try to look Amish when you are Powwowing, as this would probably end up coming across as silly or insulting. Just be yourself. Don't force anything. The more serious you take your Powwowing, the more serious your clients will take you.

For now, let's get started with the foundation of Powwow practice; healing.

The Powwow Grimoire

S	A	T	O	R
A	R	E	P	O
T	E	N	E	T
O	P	E	R	A
R	O	T	A	S

Chapter Two

The Healing Arts

The ability to soothe burns, remove warts, get rid of childhood illnesses, ease suffering, and fight diseases, are the skills that Powwow is most famous for in Pennsylvania. Many of the cures and charms were born out of a time when the scientific community was practically nonexistent and healing methods were all experimentation (many often horrendous and barbaric by today's standards). Some of the cures found in Powwow's source material are downright horrid and dangerous, yet others have stood the test of time. Here in Pennsylvania, it is not at all unusual to know someone who was taken to a Powwow as a youngster for some illness or malady that their parents couldn't explain. Certainly access to a licensed physician was rare back in the day and so the Powwow was all they had. There are some stories where the Powwow is almost elevated to mythical status for his ability to heal.

The power to heal is no small thing, and a Powwow understands that he may very well be unable to perform more than a single healing charm successfully. We must look at the issue seriously and honestly if we are to hope to gain any success. In order to heal using the charms as found within Powwow, it's crucial that you not only understand what you are saying, but the powers and energies that are invoked by saying the words. Even the most cursory glance at any of the works Powwow draws its inspiration from (Long Lost Friend, Albertus Magnus, Romanusbuchlein) will reveal that it is a Christian-inspired and empowered tradition meant for Christians to utilize. Indeed, the baptismal name of your client is required for many of the charms to work. A second consideration is an understanding of how to actually work the charms. Over the years, the largest complaint that comes to my ears from would-be Powwowers is that the Grimoires do not give direction for the use of the charms. The truth is, they DO offer instruction, if you are looking properly. However, because this is a book about how to actually perform Powwowing techniques, I have done the work for you.

In Long Lost Friend, several clues peppered throughout the book actually offer us full instruction for use of the charms. Whether this was intentionally done by Hohman or not remains a mystery. I am inclined to believe that Hohman didn't use even a small percentage of the charms he included in the LLF. Rather, he copied word-for-word many of the charms directly from Albertus Magnus. If they happened to contain some clues as to their use, it was entirely accidental on Hohman's part. I do believe he was a practitioner, but my theory about his work is just that, a theory, and there's no way for me to truly know his intentions.

The methods employed by a Powwower when performing a healing varied from practitioner to practitioner, but a few commonalities have been handed down for the past two hundred plus years...

The use of a spoken component. Most often, this was whispered or muttered so as to be unintelligible to the individual receiving the healing, and practically impossible to hear by anyone who may happen to be nearby. The spoken components come to us from the heavily Judeo-Christian Grimoires from which *Long Lost Friend* was sourced. Some words and phrases are direct quotes from scripture. Others, the majority in fact, are creative plays on Biblical themes. I suspect that at least part of the reason why we have such creative and colorful spoken charms is due to the fact that many common folk were illiterate and created prayers and charms based on their own limited knowledge of the Bible. Many of the charms were likely passed down from one individual to the next with no written counterpart, thus inevitably resulting in changes over time. At the end of the day, we can only assume with little or no actual verifiable data why the words are what they are. Needless to say, the charms are unusual at times and downright ridiculous at other times. But there you go.

By reading through Hohman we can deduce that charms are repeated a total of three times; generally twice on one day and a third time the following day. This is an unusual practice, and quite possibly it made more sense back in Hohman's time. However, tradition is tradition and if a charm calls for a third repetition the following day, so be it. In a specific charm for removing pain, Hohman instructs *"Everything prescribed in this book must be used three times…..words are always to have an interval of half an hour, and between the second third time should pass a whole night, except where it is otherwise directed."* For some variation, *Albertus Magnus* simply offers the instruction to speak the charms three times, with no indication of intervals of time or the passing of a night.

The other long-standing debate is whether or not charms are meant to be whispered. Some sources say that charms must always, as a matter of practice, be whispered. I can find no authoritative source for this in any of the written works on the subject. Indeed, the source material we do have says something quite different...

In Hohman, we find the very first charm, titled "A Charm for Hysterics". In addition to the gestures (which we will get to shortly) we are directed to "speak the following at the same time". Next, for a remedy to stop bleeding, we are instructed that *"no matter how far a person be away, if only his first name is rightly pronounced..."* In a later remedy for worms, we are only instructed to "repeat" the spoken charm three times, with no mention of whispering or muttering. And finally, in *Albertus Magnus*, the instructions for using the charms are thus: *"Whenever said remedy is to be applied....is called aloud three times with devotion."*

My analysis of the whisper debate is that, unless otherwise directed, the charms are meant to be spoken aloud, but I also believe it's a matter of personal choice. It is possible that whispering came about during a time when some individuals couldn't remember all the proper words to a charm due to illiteracy so they felt more comfortable whispering. It is also possible that some purposely whispered so as to avoid sharing their secrets with their clients. The bottom line is that it is entirely up to you if you will whisper or speak aloud. You must feel comfortable and confident with what you are doing.

Gestures and hand movements. This commonality amongst charms is also universal throughout the tradition of Powwow. Some have described the movements to be reminiscent of mesmerism techniques right out of the spiritualist movement of the 1800's. However, sweeping gestures of a sort can be found in almost every healing modality. Again, I look to Hohman for instruction here.

For a remedy for horses, the instructions include *"You must shake the head of the horse three times, and pass your hands over his back three times to and fro."* In a later remedy for stopping blood Hohman writes *"Everything prescribed for man in this book is also applicable to animals."* We can only assume that the reverse is also true, and so the instructions for passing your hands over the body "three times to and fro" must also be true for men.

Later we see instruction for ending a working by marking the sign of the cross over the affected area three times. *"It is the safest way in all these cases to make the crosses with the hand or thumb three times over the affected parts."* When you see the three crosses included in the charm (+ + +) then you are instructed to mark the crosses with the hand or thumb over the area being treated.

From the bits and pieces we can put together from Hohman and Albertus Magnus, the charms are to follow this outline:

Speak the words aloud (at your comfort level) one time, wait for a space of a half hour then repeat. Then repeat for a third time the next day. Following the spoken piece, if so directed, you are to make the sign of the three crosses over the affected area with your hand or thumb. This is done in the names of "The Father, the Son, and the Holy Ghost".

The Powwow Grimoire

S	A	T	O	R
A	R	E	P	O
T	E	N	E	T
O	P	E	R	A
R	O	T	A	S

While speaking the spoken words, the hands are to be passed over the body three times (to and fro) unless otherwise directed.

I would like to add a section here about whether or not the charms will actually work for you. My advice is this: Try them. They will either work or they will not. It is believed by the hardcore traditionalists that you absolutely must be taught the charms by another practitioner in order for them to work. That seems rather limiting to me and makes our Grimoire sources rather obsolete, doesn't it? No, I actually believe we are meant to utilize the charms. So the best way to find out if they work is to just do them. They won't be instant miracle cures. Remember, it is God affecting the healing. You just do the charm with the understanding that you are not directing energy, you are just "trying" and leaving it up to God to do the rest. It will happen or it will not, but all you can do is "try".

What follows here are some healing charms as they appear in the old sources (Long Lost Friend, Albertus Magnus, Romanus) as well as some from my own collection and additional sources that have been taught to me over the years. I did not include every single healing charm that is out there because I don't use every single healing charm.

Remember to follow the outline above for using the charms and be sure to follow any other specific directions. And please remember that when you see this (+ + +) you are to say "In the name of the Father, the Son, and the Holy Ghost" while drawing three crosses with your hand..

To Stop Blood

As Christ was born in Bethlehem and baptized in the river Jordan, he said to the water *"Be still"*. So shall thy blood cease to flow. + + +

For the sting of a bee

Hummler, Brummler, do not sting

Until the Devil's benediction bring!

To cure burns

To draw fire, pass your hand over the exposed burn, open and palm down, in a direction away from you and away from the patient, as if pushing the fire away from both you and the patient's body. Do this slowly three times, at the same time blowing gently on the burn. The head remains fixed over the burn, but turns so that your breath follows your hand thus blowing the fire away from the victim's body. Simultaneously, and each of the three times you do the above, repeat the secret healing verse. This verse must be memorized word for word, for one mistake will invalidate the cure.

There came an angel from the east

Bringing frost and fire.

In frost out fire.

+ + +

S	A	T	O	R
A	R	E	P	O
T	E	N	E	T
O	P	E	R	A
R	O	T	A	S

For Splinters

Christ was of a virgin born

And crowned was he with a crown of thorn

He did neither swell nor rebel

And I hope this never will.

At the same time, the middle finger of the right hand must be kept in motion round the thorn, and at the end of the words three times repeated, the thorn should be touched each time with the tip of the finger. Then, with God's blessing, it will give no further trouble.

For Sprains

Tie nine knots in black wool thread. Tie the thread around the sprained area. Say:

The Lord rode

And the foal slipped

He lighted,

And she righted,

Set joint to joint,

Bone to bone,

And sinew to sinew,

Heal in the Holy Ghost's name

For Burns

Three wise men came from the east

One brought fire, two carried frost.

Out fire! In frost!

In the name of the Father, Son, and Holy Ghost.

For inflammation

Lay a red handled knife across the swollen area. Repeat

three times

Across the red landscape I saw a red forest

And in the red forest I saw a red church

And in the red church I saw a red altar

And on the red altar I saw a red book

And on the red book I saw a red knife

And with the red knife I put out the inflammation!

+ + +

Plunge the knife into the earth to release the inflammation

To Stop Blood

There stood three roses upon our savior's grave. The first is mild, the other is good, the third shall stop the blood. + + +

To Drive Away Fever

Write the following order of letters (next page), sew them into a patch, hang it about the neck until the fever leaves.

AbaxaCatabax

AbaxaCataba

AbaxaCatab

AbaxaCata

AbaxaCat

AbaxaCa

AbaxaC

Abaxa

Abax

Aba

Ab

A

This charm is a variation of the ABRACADABRA charm, of Hebrew origin. It translates as "I speak the power here" or "I speak power into creation".

To cure a person or animal of worms (germs)

You are a little worm, not entirely grown

You plague me in marrow and bone

You may be white, black, or red,

In a quarter of an hour you will be dead. + + +

For wounds and stopping of blood

Blessed is the day on which Jesus Christ was born

Blessed is the day on which Jesus Christ died;

Blessed is the day on which Jesus Christ arose from the dead.

These are the three holy house; by these N.N., I stop thy blood.

Thy sores shall neither swell nor fester; no more shall that happen,

That that the Virgin Mary will bear another son.

+ + +

The Powwow Grimoire

S A T O R
A R E P O
T E N E T
O P E R A
R O T A S

To Remove Skin infections

Many of the old charms refer to a skin infection known as "wildfire". This referred to a very specific skin condition called erysipelas. Nowadays the term is used in a charm to refer to any skin irritant.

With a red string, pull it tight between your two hands. First touch the top of the individual's head then sweep the string down the front of the body and away from the person three times while you repeat the following:

Wildfire fly, fly, fly

The red string chase you away, away, away + + +

To Stop Bleeding

Hold a small rounded stone over the wound and say

The water is mud and run's aflood and so does thy blood.

God bade it stand and so it did. + + +

Another for stopping blood

Hold a red handled knife over the bleeding area while repeating:

Three ladies came from Jordan's land

Each with a bloody knife in her hand.

Stand blood stand, in the name of God stand

Bloody wound, in God's name mend! + + +

Interesting charm and its language variations

This was shared with me by a member of my church as she learned it as a child,

Heile, heal, hinkeldreck! Marifree Sicht olles weg

Or, another variation,

Heile, heile, hinkeldreck! Morgen früh ist alles weg (recht)

S	A	T	O	R
A	R	E	P	O
T	E	N	E	T
O	P	E	R	A
R	O	T	A	S

And, in English,

Holy, holy, chicken dirt. Early morning it is gone/away/right.

And, made to rhyme…

Holy, holy, chicken dirt. Tomorrow morning it won't hurt!

It is said that to spit on the area of pain helps seal the magic.

Before I move forward to the next section, I felt it was appropriate to speak a few words about some of the elements of certain charms found within the tradition and their Biblical origins.

It is a well-known fact that the color red is a color that is associated with Powwow. This comes to us from Old Testament Hebrew mysticism. In the book of genesis, we see the color red first mentioned in the story of Judah and his daughter-in-law Tamar:

When the time came for her to give birth, there were twin boys in her womb. As she was giving birth, one of them put out his hand; so the midwife took a scarlet thread and tied it on his wrist and said "This one came out first." Genesis 38:27-28

In Hebrew folklore, we also find the use of a red thread tied around an infant's wrist as a means of protecting against a sort of demon called lilitu.

The color red features prominently as a symbol for the blood of the sacrifice, which is mentioned more times in the Bible than we have room for here. In addition, the Israelites are spared the wrath of God by marking their doorways in blood, as follows:

They are to take some of the blood and put it on the sides and tops of the door frames of the houses where they eat the lambs.... On that same night I will pass through Egypt and strike down every firstborn - and I will bring judgment on all the gods of Egypt.... The blood will be a sign for you on the houses where you are; and when I see the blood, I will pass over you. No destructive plague will touch you when I strike Egypt.... Exodus 12:7, 12-13

In fact, many Powwow charms invoke the power of Jesus' blood. In those charms, it would be appropriate to utilize red string in some way as a part of the gestures for your healing.

The following entry from Long Lost Friends is not actually a charm at all. Rather, it is an indication that the creator of this particular passage is recommending the Bible as a means to remedy "bad wounds and burns". the Bible, though not specifically mentioned as a prop to use in many of the charms, has historically been a part of Powwowing practice. Most Powwow Doctors interviewed on the topic over the years have indicated that they use their Bible in their Powwowing practice.

A good remedy for bad wounds and burns

The word of God, the milk of Jesus' mother, and Christ's blood, is for all wounds and burnings good.

To remove pain and heal up wounds with three switches

With this switch and Christ's dear blood, I banish your pain and do you good. + + +

Remedy for fever, worms, and the colic

Jerusalem, thou Jewish city, in which Christ our Lord was born; thou shalt turn into water and blood, because it is for (name's) fever, worms, and colic good. + + +

Red has been used by the church over the centuries a favorite paint color for the main entrance doors. There are two reasons for this. The first and most recent meaning is to mimic the doors of Wittenberg Cathedral in Germany where Martin Luther posted his 95 Theses, which were red. The second explanation is that in Christian mysticism, red is the color of sanctuary and refuge, and all churches are supposed to be places of safety and sanctuary. This is in tune with the belief that red symbolizes the blood of Christ and that all who pass through that blood, or are 'cleansed' by it, are symbolically and mystically entering the body of Christ.

Occasionally, a Powwow remedy or charm may seem like nonsense or gibberish. In some cases, we can dissect the charm into its various components to figure it out. Let's take the following charm as an example.

The Powwow Grimoire

S	A	T	O	R
A	R	E	P	O
T	E	N	E	T
O	P	E	R	A
R	O	T	A	S

A good remedy for the fever

Good morning, dear Thursday! Take away from (name) the 77-fold fevers. Oh! Thou dear Lord Jesus Christ, take them away from him! + + +

This must be used on Thursday for the first time, on Friday for the second time, and on Saturday for the third time; and each time thrice. The prayer of faith has also to be said each time, and not a word dare be spoken to anyone until the sun has risen. Neither dare the sick person speak to anyone till after sunrise; nor eat pork, nor drink milk, nor cross a running water, for nine days.

This is one of my favorite charms, simply because it is so heavily filled with Biblical symbolism and mysticism. Let's take it apart and see.

Good morning dear Thursday! ... used on a Thursday for the first time.... Why Thursday? Traditionally, the Last Supper is thought to have taken place on Thursday. Afterward, Jesus went to the Garden of Gethsemane to pray and was arrested shortly after. Thursday is seen as a Holy Day for this reason.

77-fold….. the number seven, and multiples of it, are repeated countless times throughout the Bible. In the Gospel of Matthew, we see this account in the Parable of the Unmerciful Servant.

Then Peter came to Jesus and asked, "Lord, how many times shall I forgive my brother or sister who sins against me? Up to seven times?" Jesus answered, "I tell you, not seven times, but seventy-seven times" (Matthew 18)

In Luke, we see that there are 77 generations from Adam to Jesus. And in Genesis, Lamek is avenged 77 times.

"The prayer of faith…" this is in reference to a truly heartfelt pleas to God, with full faith that God will not only hear your prayer, but he will answer it. We find this in many places in the Bible, but

this specific phrasing comes to us from James 5:15:

And the prayer offered in faith will make the sick person

well; the Lord will raise them up. If they have sinned, they

will be forgiven.

"Nor eat port, nor drink milk..." these are straight from Old

Testament Judaic laws. There are many food-related laws in the Old

Testament that give instruction as to clean and unclean things to

eat. Certain things should never be mixed together, and other

restrictions apply. These instructions speak of the Judaic influence

insofar as fasting and dietary restriction during the period of

healing.

"Not a word dare be spoken to anyone until after the sun

has risen..." There are instructions within this charm for both the

Powwow Doctor and the sick person to adhere to. Neither can

speak to anyone until after sunrise on all three days the charm is worked. This is no easy feat! Within Powwow, these detailed instructions are often ignored by practitioners, or charms of this nature are skipped because of their complexity. I believe it is important for us to stick with these instructions so that we can gain the maximum benefit of using these particular charms.

As a healer, you will eventually learn which charms work best for you, which have mild success, and which don't work at all. Every Powwower is different. Indeed, if you look at the historical powwow, you'll find that often the powwower was known for his ability to heal one or two different things, and that's it. Nowadays we have more information to work with so we can try our hands at many different charms. As I stated earlier; they will either work for you or they will not. Even the most experienced of us have an even blend of successes and failures. It just is what it is. Your job is to work the charm and leave it up to God to do the rest. Don't put pressure on yourself and don't force it. Just do the charm. That's all you can do.

If a client comes to you for healing, be sure to follow the traditional practice of asking them if they believe in God. This is certainly not a Politically Correct question, but it is a traditional aspect of Powwowing. The client's belief, or non-belief, may very well make or break a powwowing session. If they believe, then ask them their baptismal name. Then you work the charm. Then you send them home. I definitely would not recommend turning it into a social event. Don't follow up the session with coffee and donuts or, even worse, mixed cocktails and party food. Just do what you do and send them on their way. If the charm requires you to follow up the next day, then do so. If there are special instructions with the charm, such as the previously mentioned charm, then let the person know as you are walking them out your door.

I learned a long time ago that to become too chummy with your clients opens the door for all sorts of negativity. It was after learning this lesson that I started seeing clients on my front porch and not allowing them inside. Eventually, I stopped allowing clients at my home at all. The best advice I can offer you is to either meet

The Powwow Grimoire

S	A	T	O	R
A	R	E	P	O
T	E	N	E	T
O	P	E	R	A
R	O	T	A	S

them in their home or somewhere neutral but private, do your charm, then end the meeting.

Before I continue onto the next chapter, I just want to say that this information that I've provided is quite possibly more than a majority of what the historical powwow would have practiced. Simple healing charms were the norm in Powwowing. Some delved outside that norm, but not all. If you were to stop right here and read no further, you would have more Powwowing information than a lot of folks. You could work with these few healing charms for the rest of your life and build a reputation as you gain more practice and confidence.

These healing charms are by no means the sum totality of what Powwowing has to offer. However, they are a good variety and will give you plenty to work with as you begin Powwowing for clients. For more healing charms, visit my website www.PAGermanPowwow.com.

Chapter Three

Protection Charms

The Powwowing source materials have a fantastic array of protective charms and talismans for you to work with. There are protective charms for everything from angry dogs to bullets. You can find charms to protect from thieves, witches, misfortune, and accidental poisoning. If a client comes to you and they are in need of protection of some type, you would generally work the protective charm on your own, without your client present. This may require you to actually craft some form of talisman or write something on paper or perform other actions that your client need not know about. The important thing here is to tell your client that you will get back to them, then you can plan when and how you will do your protective work. Some charms may require you to wait until a certain moon phase or day of the week. You may have your own personal preferences for when/how you do your protective work. Your client does not need to know all of your little details, but they should respect your practice enough to accept that you will get back to them when the time is right. Of course, you may give them something to do on their own in the meantime, should you feel the situation warrants it. It's entirely up to you.

As always, use common sense with protective work. If you feel your client needs police intervention in their life, tell them so. You can still do your work for them, but they need to be smart and logical about their situation. No one should rely solely on a Powwow if their life is in danger.

To insure safety from an angry dog

Put your right hand out, palm down, and gesture three times softly while saying

Dog, hold thy nose to the ground;

God has made me and thee, hound. + + +

A Protective Talisman

To be hung in the home, hidden in a secret place, or carried with you.

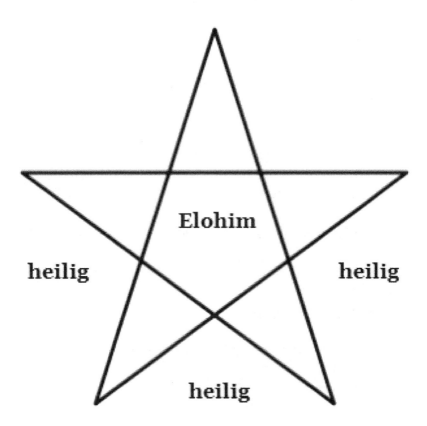

A charm to make a thief return stolen goods

Write upon two pieces of paper the following words, and attach one to the top of the door, and the other under the threshold and the thief will return on the third day and bring back the stolen articles:

Abraham born it +

Isaac redeemed and found it +

Jacob carried it home +

It is bound as tightly as steel and iron, chains and fetters +

To protect the home

Go to each window and door individually. In the air make the sign of the cross while saying:

Three angels with three swords stand before the house of God.

The first is courage

The second is strength

The third strikes down all enemies

+ + +

To banish all robbers, murderers, and foes

The following is written on parchment then rolled up and hidden inside the barn or garage.

God be with you, brethren. Desist you, thieves, robbers, murderers, way layers, and warriors in meekness, because we all have partaken of the rose-colored blood of Jesus Christ. Your rifles, guns, and cannons be spiked, with the holy drops of our Redeemer's blood. All sabers and deadly weapons be closed, with the five wounds of our dear Master, Jesus Christ. Three roses are blooming on Jesus' heart. The first is kind, the other is mighty, the third represents God's strong will. Under these, ye thieves and murderers are become still, as long as I will, and ye are banished, and your foul deeds have vanished.

For general protection

The following is drawn on paper or painted on a wooden disk or ceramic plate and either carried or placed in the home. This charm is believed to protect against all misfortunes, accidents, witchcraft, the devil, and fire. It is said that if you draw this on a plate and toss it onto a fire, the flames will be extinguished (I can't personally verify this).

$$\textbf{SATOR}$$
$$\textbf{AREPO}$$
$$\textbf{TENET}$$
$$\textbf{OPERA}$$
$$\textbf{ROTAS}$$

To create a protective circle around your home

Fill a large glass jar with fresh water. Say over the water 77 times:

Adonai, Elohim, the Lord my God

Pour the water on the ground around the perimeter of your home.

To Prevent Weak or Malicious Persons from doing you an injury

On a piece of paper, write the following:

Dullix, ix, ux. Yea, you can't come over Pontio; Pontio is above Pilato. + + +

Hang this above the main entrance to your house.

To secure one's self against wicked people whilst traveling, and being in danger of being attacked.

Speak three times: *Two wicked eyes have overshadowed me, but three other eyes are overshadowing me too, the one of God the Father, the other of God the Son, the third of God the Holy Spirit, they watch my blood and flesh, my marrow and bone, and all other*

large and small limbs, they shall be protected in the name of God.

+ + +

To banish a person

For this charm, you must instruct the client to collect a handful of dirt from the intended person's footprint. This may require some time and skill on their part, but if they are serious about this then they will do it. When the dirt is collected, you can assure them that you will let them know when your work is finished and send them on their way. During a dark moon, take the dirt to a crossroads chosen for your Powwowing work and stand in the center. Toss the dirt in all four directions beginning West, then South, then East, then North while saying:

The eyes of God the Father, God the Son, and God the Holy

Spirit watch your steps. Evildoer, your actions are overshadowed by the power of Christ's blood. In the three holy names I scatter you to

the four winds. + + +

S	A	T	O	R
A	R	E	P	O
T	E	N	E	T
O	P	E	R	A
R	O	T	A	S

Chapter Four

Hexerei; the practice of witchcraft

Hex (from the Oxford English dictionary)

VERB

North American

Cast a spell on; bewitch.

'he hexed her with his fingers'

NOUN

North American

A magic spell; a curse.

'a death hex'

A witch.

Origin

Mid 19th century (as a verb): from Pennsylvanian German hexe (verb), Hex (noun), from German hexen (verb), Hexe (noun).

Here in Pennsylvania, the subject of witchcraft is taken quite seriously. Prior to the arrival of the Wicca movement in the late 1960's, the word "witch" was used to describe someone who primarily worked malevolent magic. Witches were believed to be agents of the Devil.

But sometimes, the word "hex" was used to describe a Powwower. There are some who believe that Powwowers were not afraid to cross ethical lines, should the situation dictate its necessity. And indeed, some of the charms in the old Powwowing Grimoires are downright horrid.

My research has found many examples of a Powwow being referred to as a "Hex Doctor". In large part this was from the medical community, and I believe this was all a part of their smear campaign against the more traditional folk healing remedies. In some ways, I can understand it. The world was progressing rapidly and there was a concerted effort on the part of the scientific community to bring everyone forward, whether willingly or with a lot of kicking and screaming. Many of the rural communities didn't want to give up their traditional ways, so practices like Powwow were demonized by the press and by the scientific community. It wasn't long before people began having unfavorable views of Powwowing altogether; viewing it as superstition or something to be feared or even scoffed at. It's not difficult to see how some might begin to believe that a Powwow was no longer working on the side of God but consorting with something darker...something evil.

Nowadays, the word "witch" has multiple meanings. And, to be completely honest, the word is more of a pain than anything else. For the purposes of this book and in the context of the Pennsylvania German tradition of Powwowing, the words "witch" and "hex" are meant to describe someone who is a worker of malevolent magic. That individual may very well be Joe Sunshine most of the time. But as soon as Joe Sunshine crosses those ethical lines and seeks to intentionally harm someone out of spite or malicious intent then that is *hexerei*. And that's the type of witchcraft a Powwow must combat. There are even a few rare instances in history of a Powwow who worked his healing by day in the name of Jesus Christ, but at night time worked nefarious magic in the name of the Devil. These are very rare cases, but certainly existed throughout history; as they likely do today.

Are the threats of witchcraft really and truly real? Even if we ignore the history of witchcraft in the state of Pennsylvania, it is extremely easy to determine if such a thing as "witchcraft" exists. Any of the large chain bookstores will have a section often labeled as "New Age" where books on witchcraft; historical and modern version, can be found. A large portion of the modern strain of witchcraft is nothing more than harmless "kitchen witchery" involving healing spells and simple divinatory practices, not terribly unlike Powwowing. But this type of witchcraft is beyond the scope of this book. We are discussing malevolent witchery.

A simple internet search for 'witchcraft curses' can yield some interesting results. There are countless individuals in the world that label themselves as "witches", all with varying degrees of intent. What all of this means is that yes, there are people who identify as witches and yes, there are people who use witchcraft.

If we believe we can do good, then we must also believe that we have the capacity for great evil.

Although it may be difficult to believe, I have had more people come to me over the years who believe they have been cursed than for any other reason. From these experiences I have learned several things:

1- sometimes people curse themselves, either through playing around with things they shouldn't be or because they psychologically jinx themselves with their own negativity.

2-sometimes people really have been cursed (verhexed) by a practicing witch; and in some instances they went looking for trouble and they found it!

3-sometimes people really have been cursed and they don't know why, or even who did it to them.

4-sometimes people just want some excitement in their lives, and they make stuff up.

As a Powwow, you will likely meet all four types, as well as other types that I haven't mentioned here. It's not nice to say that people are lying or pretending or creating drama, but there you go. In my experience, no matter what you may believe about the client or uncover in your questioning of them, it's really best to just work the anti-hex charm for them anyway. Let God sort it out as He will.

But how do you know what you are dealing with?

There is no hard and fast method. However, sometimes you can figure it out after a few leading questions. Here are just a few ideas for you to ask your client. It's best to get as much information as you can so you know how best to proceed. I would advise against

The Powwow Grimoire

S	A	T	O	R
A	R	E	P	O
T	E	N	E	T
O	P	E	R	A
R	O	T	A	S

telling your client you think they are lying or wrong or even that you believe they have a powerful hex on them. Just listen to them, silently analyze the situation, work the anti-hex charm, then send them on their way. Just as with healing, anti-hex work should be kept at a business level then get the person out of your house. In general, most anti-hex charms will be worked without your client present, as you will see once we get into the actual charms. So you can speak to them, make your analyses, then assure them you will do your thing and take care of the situation.

Are you experiencing frequent illness?

Are you experiencing frequent periods of "bad luck"?

Are you experiencing relationship difficulties?

Are you experiencing financial/employment difficulties?

Have you seen a medical doctor/psychologist/counselor?

Do you know why someone would target you with witchcraft?

Do you know someone who practices witchcraft?

Could your condition be self-inflicted?

The Powwow Grimoire

S	A	T	O	R
A	R	E	P	O
T	E	N	E	T
O	P	E	R	A
R	O	T	A	S

Are your pets behaving in an unusual manner?

Are you sleeping properly?

Are you having unusual or dangerous thoughts?

Do you believe in God?

There is a warning here when you ask these questions. If an individual comes to you and they are in a bad state of mind, we don't want to pry too much. The danger of asking questions like this is that maybe the person didn't think their situation was that bad, or maybe they only thought it was affecting their relationship, for example. Once you start asking questions about their dogs, their jobs, their sleep habits, etc. they may very well start super-imposing some of their anxiety onto those areas of their lives and start seeing negativity where there previously was none. We don't want to make their situation worse. So each case must be handled delicately. Remember, there are some people who are truly in tough situations and may be looking for something to blame. Try to be sympathetic, but remember that you are not a licensed therapist (unless, of course, you really are). You can suggest they talk to someone that is a professional, if you feel it will help, but be careful not to get too chummy with the client and try not to give medical or mental health advice. Just do your Powwow then send them on their way.

If you've read the earlier editions of this book then you will be surprised at how many of the charms I chose to NOT include in this updated edition. The reason for this is simple: most of those charms were useless. I included them for historical interest, but there was no real use for most of them anyway, so their addition was just taking up space. Instead, I've chosen to include charms that ARE useful, even if I don't agree with using some of them.

A few things to remember about the charms.

N.N. or N. Signify the use of a name; either your own or your client's. This typically refers to the Baptismal name.

JJJ signifies the name Jesus, spoken three times.

INRI is the Latin inscription *Jesus Nazarenus Rex Iudaeorum*... Jesus of Nazareth, King of the Jews.

+ + + means you should make three crosses over the person or affected area while saying "In the name of the Father, the Son, and the Holy Ghost."

I leave it to you to use whichever charms you see fit to use, at your own risk of crossing personal or religious ethical lines. In some cases, you may need to teach the charm to your client so that they can perform it on their own. You'll need to analyze each situation to determine what is most appropriate.

To bind a witch so that she is unable to take action against you.

On parchment, write the offending witch's full name. Fold the paper three times and bind with red string while saying:

Then I saw an angel coming down from heaven, having the key to the bottomless pit and a great chain in his hand. He laid hold of the dragon, that serpent of old, who is the Devil and Satan, and bound him for a thousand years; and he cast him into the bottomless pit, and shut him up, and set a seal on him, so that he should deceive the nations no more till the thousand years were finished.

The bound paper is placed inside a box. On the box is written **INRI**

Seal the box and bury in a churchyard. The witch will be unable to attack you again.

To cause the powers of the witch to return upon him/her

In a glass jar, place three iron nails, shards from a broken mirror, and urine of the one effected. Add stones enough to fill the jar and increase its weight. Seal tightly. Place in a swiftly flowing river. The witch will never be able to effect you and his curses will rebound upon him.

To bind a witch and cause him grief

Three iron nails must be hammered into the left foot print of a witch on his own property. The nails are pounded in the names of the Holy Trinity. A bit of dirt is collected from the foot print and buried in the north side of a churchyard. The witch will be unable to act and will find frustration at every attempt.

If a human being or beast is attacked by evil spirits, how to restore him and make him well again

Thou arch-sorcerer, thou has attached N.N.; let that witchcraft recede from him into thy marrow and into thy bone, let it be returned unto thee. I exorcise thee for the sake of the five wounds of Jesus, thou evil spirit, and conjure thee for the fibe wounds of Jesus of this flesh, marrow and bone; I exorcise thee for the sake of the five wounds of Jesus, at this very hour restore to health again N.N. in the name of God the Father, God the Son, and of God the Holy Spirit. + + +

If a man or beast is attacked by wicked people, a means of banishing them

Bedgoblin and all ye evil spirits, I forbid you my bedstead, my couch; I forbid you, in the name of God, my house and home; I forbid you, in the name of the Holy Trinity, my blood and flesh, my body and soul; I forbid you all the nail holes in my house and home, till you have traveled over every hillock, waded through every water, have counted all the leaflets of the trees, and counted all the starlets in the sky, until that beloved day arrives when the mother of God will bring forth her second Son. + + +

To know when cattle or other animals are plagued by witches

The hair stands on end, or bristles on the head, and they generally sweat by night or near dawn of day.

When a man or cattle is plagued by witches or ill-disposed persons

Go on Good Friday, or Golden Sunday, before the sun rises, to a hazelnut bush, cut a stick therefrom with a sympathetic weapon, by making three cuts above the hand toward the rise of the sun, in the name of the Holy Trinity. Carry the stick quietly into the house, conceal it so that no one can get hold of it. When a man or beast is plagued by evil disposed people, walk three times around such a haunted person, while pronouncing the three holiest names; after this proceeding, take off thy hat and hit it with the stick and thus you smite the wicked being.

Note: The above charm can be useful if you make the stick on Good Friday and keep it in a secretive place to be used exclusively for this charm. Because the charm calls for the use of your hat, I would suggest wearing a hat when you work this charm.

To beat witches

Note: this charm is designed to cause physical harm to the witch. I include it here as a matter of historical interest. I leave it to you to decide if you wish to cross personal ethical lines.

Let the sweepings, which are swept together in a house for three days, remain in a heap. On the third day, cover it with a black cloth. Then take the stick of an elm tree and flog the dirt heap. If the witch does not come to you to confess or apologize, this charm

supposedly causes the witch to be beaten to death.

To Burn a witch so that she receives pock marks over her entire body

Note: here is another charm designed to cause harm. Use at your

own risk.

Take butter and melt in an iron pan. Add ivy or wintergreen

and fry it. Take three nails of a coffin and place in the mixture. Carry

the mixture to a place where neither sun nor moon can shine and

pour it there. The witch will be sick with pock marks for half a year.

Further note: this charm does not specify is the mixture should be

poured on to something that represents the witch or if one should

speak the witch's name while making the mixture. I have no further

advice to offer as I have never attempted this charm.

The Powwow Grimoire

S	A	T	O	R
A	R	E	P	O
T	E	N	E	T
O	P	E	R	A
R	O	T	A	S

To cut a stick wherewith one can flog someone however distant

Take note when the moon becomes new on a Tuesday, then go before sunrise, step up to a stick which you have selected beforehand, stand facing the sunrise and speak these words "Stick, I grasp you in the names of God the Father, God the Son, and God the Holy Ghost." Take your knife in your hand and speak again "Stick, I cut you in the names of God the Father, God the Son, and God the Holy Ghost that you be obedient to me, and flog whom I wish to flog, when I speak their name." Afterwards, place cuts in two places on the stick, somewhat apart, so that you can write between them **ABIA OBIE, TABIA**. When you want to use the stick, place your coat or hat over a shear heap or a pile of clippings from another animal. Strike the coat or hat with the stick and call the person's name who you wish to flog. Supposedly, they will feel the blows.

Chapter Five

Herbal remedies

Even though gardens and farms are not quite as prevalent as they were 100 years ago, some Powwowers still embrace the old herbal remedies that most of us learned from our parents or grandparents. In the Pennsylvania German culture, many of our almanacs still contain articles about herbal remedies and other popular do-it-yourself cures that utilize components found in most gardens. What follows is by no means a comprehensive listing of uses for herbs. My disclaimer is that you should always research methods such as this on your own, talk to your doctor, and seek proper medical attention when necessary.

I've categorized the herbs by their usage.

Alteratives: medicines that correct a condition by targeting the blood (as a blood cleanser). This is one of the most common types of herbal remedies. Some of the best and most potent

Alteratives include; spikenard root, yellow dock, red clover, burdock root, dandelion root, sarsaparilla bark, goldenseal root, and elderberry flower.

Antibiotics: medicines that target harmful micro-organisms and infections. One of the most powerful antibiotic herbals is garlic. Garlic can be eaten raw or cooked and can be added to any number of dishes to both enhance the flavor and to function as a natural antibiotic. Antibiotics target the harmful organisms in our body and also help cleanse away what is known as 'free radicals', which are germs and organisms we pick up throughout the course of a normal day. Parsley is another popular antibiotic and should be chewed (fresh sprigs) with your meal.

Antihelmintics: herbals that destroy worms and parasites. Garlic is also a powerful antihelmintic; as is wormwood, male fern root, elm bark, flax seed, Jerusalem oak, pumpkin seed, pomegranate rind, and spigelia root. Ground coconut husk and tansy flowers are also effective. It is recommended that a physician be consulted in all cases of worms and parasites.

Antipyretics: these are medicines which prevent or reduce fevers. Calamus root, golden seal, balsam poplar, and witch-grass are the most common; as are feverfew, sweet birch, and wintergreen.

Antirheumatics: these are medicines that reduce swelling in the joints; effective for arthritis. Natural oils are the most effective for this condition such as oils of wintergreen, rhododendron, and even poison ivy. Oils can be expensive so often natural pain relievers are sought after, such as willow bark.

Antiscorbutics: herbal medicines for preventing or curing scurvy (lack of Vitamin C). Citrus plants (fruits and vegetables) are sources of vitamin C and can be eaten to counteract scurvy. Rose Hip tea is also a great source. Blending Rose Hips with oranges (in a chopper) and making a juice is a tasty and healthy combat for scurvy.

Antispasmodics: herbs that relieve spasms, contractions, muscle tension, and some headaches. These include skullcap, chamomile, hop flowers, purslane, and mint. Red raspberry leaves are also popular.

Antiseptics: medicines preventing mortification and infection. Alcohol-based tinctures work best. Sassafrass, boneset, elecampane, and persimmon bark are the best.

Aperients: herbal laxatives. These include witch-grass, burdock, chicory, blue flag, elderberry, dandelion, and violets (made into infusions).

Astringents: herbs that are used as washes and rinses to cleanse of germs and bacteria. Agrimony, alum, bayberry, black cherry, black willow bark, kola nuts, logwood, sage, uva ursi leaves, witch hazel, and blackberry root, are just a few of the most common herbals with astringent properties. You can steep the fresh herb in an already existing astringent liquid (such as mouthwash) to increase its effectiveness.

Bitters: herbs used to stimulate appetite. Typically taken in small doses as an infusion. Common herbs include barberry root, bayberry leaves, chamomile flowers, dandelion root, gentian root, mugwort, serpentaria root, wild cherry bark, and wormwood.

Calmatives: medicines that have a calming effect. These include catnip, chamomile, fennel seed, hops, linden flowers, orange flowers, valerian, passion flower, and celery seed.

Demulcents: herbs used to create a soothing lubrication such as cough syrups. These include arrow root, comfrey root, flaxseed, gum Arabic, irish moss, licorice root, marshmallow root, okra pods, oatmeal, and slippery elm bark.

Emetics: herbals that induce vomiting. These include dogbane, swamp milkweed, blessed thistle, scotch broom, wild yam, colic root, boneset, blue flag, vervain, and lobelia. Please consult a health care professional before preparing an emetic.

The Powwow Grimoire

S	A	T	O	R
A	R	E	P	O
T	E	N	E	T
O	P	E	R	A
R	O	T	A	S

Expectorants: herbs used to stimulate the secretion of saliva and the expulsion of phlegm. These include spikenard, poplar buds, bloodroot, sassafrass, coltsfoot, horehound, elecampane, ipecac, licorice root, wild ginger, and yerba santa.

Laxatives: herbs that stimulate evacuation of intestines and bowels. Should be used only under the order of a proper physician. These include cascara bark, golden seal, senna pods, gentian, yellow root, butternut bark, turtlebloom, licorice root, dandelion root, and peach tree leaves.

This is by no means an exhaustive or all-inclusive herbal guide. However, this information is more than enough to get your started with herbal remedies, should you choose to incorporate this aspect into your Powwowing.

There are various methods for using herbs. They include poultices, infusions, tinctures, infused oils, and salves.

Poultices: are made by bruising and smashing the leaves of the chosen plant to extract its juices. These are generally moistened with a little water to enhance the effect. Poultices are typically placed directly on the skin.

Tinctures: are made by soaking fresh or ground herbs in clear vodka to extract the healing properties. This mixture should be allowed to soak for several weeks. When finished, a tincture should be double strained to remove all traces of the plant. The tincture is then stored in a cool, dark place for up to a year.

Infused Oils: are made by soaking your chosen herbals in an oil, such as sunflower or vegetable oil. The oil will dissolve the herbal and thus become infused with the important properties. Infused oils are generally rubbed on the skin. In rarer cases, with safe herbs, they can be used for cooking.

Salves: are made by adding two tablespoons of melted beeswax into one cup of infused oil. Blend well and let congeal into a salve. These do not last long, several weeks at the most.

Infusions: are the most common, and easiest, herbal remedies. Bruise or crush the fresh herb and place in a cup. Add boiling water, cover the cup with a saucer, and let steep for about 15 minutes. Strain if desired. Drink. Infusions should be made-to-order.

If you choose to grow your own herbs, I would recommend consulting a good almanac that discusses your local climate and planting conditions.

Chapter Six

Hex Signs and Himmelsbriefs

Hex signs are the signature folk art of the Pennsylvania Germans. Hex signs dot the countryside from Berks County to York County, and all places in between. They are typically the first thing that comes to mind when you mention the Pennsylvania Germans or, as most people know us as, the Pennsylvania "Dutch".

Hex signs have an interesting reputation as being talismans of power, magic, protection, anti-witchcraft, and a whole slew of other things. However, the origins of hex signs are really quite simple: they were decorative barn art. They began as simple stars and flowers and eventually evolved into the beautiful works of art we have today.

In the early part of the last century, the tourism industry cashed in on the barn artwork and the hex sign industry was born. As time moved forward, the artists began associating meanings with the symbols and colors and now we have the talismanic uses that they are most famous for.

Let me just interject here that hex signs actually have nothing to do with Powwowing. They are a piece of folk art. However, because talismanic meanings have been assigned to them in recent years, I've chosen to include a small section here, just in case you want to try your hand at creating a few signs for yourself.

Known as the Grand Daddy of Hexes, this hex promises luck and prosperity all year round. The twelve leaves symbolize the 12 Apostles, the 12 months, and the 12 signs of the zodiac.

The tulip petals signify faith and hope.

This dynamic hex offers protection year round as well as smooth

sailing through life.

The Welcome hex features two distlefinks, signs of luck and

blessing.

Love and romance and happiness are the themes of this hex.

The lucky stars and the 12-pointed rosette offer protection and

luck.

Another version of the welcome hex with a focus on a loving

relationship.

The House Blessing hex can bring peace and God's blessing into

your home.

The Tree of Life encourages a strong family, protection, and luck.

Faith, hope, love, and charity.

Himmelsbriefs

The word *Himmelsbrief* translates as "letter from Heaven". It is a hand-written note or letter offering protection to the bearer. Many examples of early 20th century *Himmelsbriefs* can be found decorating homes or hanging in antique shops. A *himmelsbrief* can be a simple note written by a Powwower promising protection or can be an elaborate work of art, decorated with fraktur and religious symbols and framed and hung in the home.

To create a *himmelsbrief*, you really just need to state your intention for the paper in your writing. A sample follows:

By the Holy Powers of God the Father, God the Son, and God the Holy Ghost, do I call upon for protection for the bearer of this letter from all acts of witchcraft, all disease, all tempests, all storms, all famines, all accidents, all injuries, and all thefts. Whosoever carries this letter on his person, as well as his

household, will be safe from all misfortunes and maladies and will be protected by the powers of God Himself, as is written in Scripture, I CALL UPON THE LORD WHO IS WORTHY TO BE PRAISED AND I AM SAVED FROM MY ENEMIES. It is declared and set forth, in the name of God the Father, God the Son, and God the Holy Ghost. Amen.

The *Himmelsbrief* can be folded and carried in a wallet or purse, it can be rolled up and tucked away inside a hiding spot inside the home or barn, or it can become a beautiful work of art to be framed. Some himmelsbriefs have been found tucked inside the family bible.

If you are planning to create a *himmelsbriefs* for someone, you may choose to keep the process simple. You can use parchment or regular paper and just state your intent in a basic prayer, as shown on the previous page.

If you'd like to add a more ritualistic element to it, you may choose to follow the instructions for creating talismans, which will be found in Chapter 8.

S A T O R
A R E P O
T E N E T
O P E R A
R O T A S

Chapter Seven

Divination

In the mid 1990's I visited a Powwow woman in Franklin County, Pennsylvania who read fortunes in playing cards. Her methods were referred to by locals as "Gypsy readings" although it is not uncommon for certain types of divination and magic to be attributed to "Gypsies", whether it originated with them or not. The practice of reading fortunes and divining the future with playing cards is reminiscent of the English occult and spiritualist movement and, indeed, I have read many stories of English Cunning Men reading for clients and receiving money in exchange for the reading.

Card reading, although not quite as popular with the Pennsylvania Germans, was not entirely unheard of. However, this should not be confused with the modern "tarot reader" that is often seen at psychic or new age fairs. Rather, the readings were done with regular playing cards and were decidedly less mysterious in nature. Personally, I fell that playing card divinatory readings possess more style and sophistication than the tarot, but that's just my personal preference.

When I visited the Powwow in Franklin County, I noted that she was an extremely religious woman. She had an office at the back of her home in which she entertained her clients. It was accessed by means of a separate entrance. There was even a small waiting room. When I arrived, I had to wait for her to finish up with another client. When that client left, I entered a small office that had two chairs and a small table. She gestured for me to be seated and asked me to place my money on the table. The cost was exactly five dollars. Once I put the money down, she snatched it up and put it somewhere out of sight then immediately her hands started throwing cards out onto the table. All the while she was speaking non-stop in a sort of trance-like state. Her words were barely coherent but were a mixture of prayers and interpretations of the cards she was laying down. Her litany ran something like this:

"The Lord God is above us and within us and blessed our lives with abundance...be on your guard for false friends and troubles with the neighbors... the Almighty protects us and renders the works of the devil to be undone... steer clear of getting yourself int rouble with the law and don't lose sight of your goals or you'll be in a world of financial trouble... and He blessed us with everlasting life so long as we accept Him as our savior... and while you are young you may feel like you have no direction, but you know what you love to do and you should figure out what you want your life to be... and God be with us all and guide us and protect us in Jesus name..."

And so it went, for about fifteen minutes. I don't remember her pausing for breath and she certainly never asked me any questions. At the time I remember thinking she was something of a crackpot, but it's only now, later in life, that I realize that there was something uniquely powerful and valid about her methods. Over the years I learned a few divination techniques of my own, but nothing seems quite as stylish to me as playing card divination. The particular meanings I learned for the cards were taught to me by a friend and Powwow practitioner. I do not know where he learned the meanings, but this system works well for me and so I present it to you, with his blessing, just as I learned it.

What follows is a simplistic form of playing card divination that you can expand upon on your own as you see fit. All you will need is a standard deck of playing cards. To do the reading, you shuffle the cards then hand them to your client to shuffle. While they are shuffling, you say a prayer for God to guide your words so that you give the advice that your client most needs to hear. Do not add your own ego into it, just interpret the cards as you see them and let the client fit it into their lives. If your message is divinely inspired, the client will hear what they need to hear.

Once the client is finished shuffling the cards, you being turning cards over. You will turn over a total of three rows of cards, three cards in each row; for a total of nine cards. The top row represents actions which have brought the client into their current condition. The middle row represents what is currently at work in the client's life. The bottom row represent advice the client needs to hear in order to move forward.

The meanings of the cards are dependent upon two factors: the suit and the number.

-**Hearts** represent love and relationships; including family, friends, and partners.

-**Clubs** represent where your client's energy is directed or should be directed.

-**Spades** represent hidden or unknown forces at work that your client should be aware of.

-**Diamonds** represent financial/monetary issues.

Ones represent beginnings, new starts, the client himself, and inspiration.

Twos represent the things we are attached to, those things which we care for.

Threes represent people in our immediate life, our siblings, our friends.

Fours represent our home, our memories, our mothers.

Fives represent those things which give us pleasure.

Sixes represent our health.

Sevens represent our intimate relationships; those we love and those who are our enemies.

The Powwow Grimoire

S	A	T	O	R
A	R	E	P	O
T	E	N	E	T
O	P	E	R	A
R	O	T	A	S

Eights represent those things in life that are unpleasant to us and we wish not to deal with.

Nines represent things we learn or pray for.

Tens represent the attainment of goals and our fathers.

Jacks represent the people in our lives that influence us.

Queens represent those that pay attention to us; for good or ill.

Kings represent those that are in authority over us; for good or ill.

Each card drawn is interpreted first by its number then by its suit and finally by its placement in the reading. For example, a Nine of Hearts in the row of cards representing the Present can mean that right now your client is hoping or praying for a relationship. Because this appeared in the reading, perhaps that is the cause of their issues. Much depends on other cards in the reading to flesh out the interpretation.

Your cards can be kept locked away when not in use, if that is your preference, or you can also use them to play Gin Rummy,..,. it is up to you to determine how best to treat your divination cards. I have learned over the years not to put too much emphasis on keeping things "sacred" because if something happens to my things, I feel a deep loss for them. But when my Powwowing tools are a part of my everyday waking life, there seems to be more power to them while at the same time less emotional attachment. But the choice is yours.

The Powwow Grimoire

S	A	T	O	R
A	R	E	P	O
T	E	N	E	T
O	P	E	R	A
R	O	T	A	S

Magic Mirrors (erdspeigel)

Within Powwow there are several variations magic mirrors used for divinatory purposes. In most cases, these mirrors are used to discern the identity of the witch who has cursed you, should you be unfortunate enough to have become the victim of hexerei. There are a few different sets of instructions these mirrors in the old Grimoires. Consensus amongst the practitioners is that a mirror must contain the following inscription in order for it to be useful:

S Solam S Tattler Echogardner Gematar

The meaning of this inscription is unclear and may very well be what is known as "barbarous' language; meaning it is nonsensical and used only for this purpose. The words may have had meaning at one time, and were poorly translated over and over again, in which case their original meaning may be lost forever.

The library of Kutztown University has record of two such mirrors in possession of writer Ann Hark. In her examples, the above inscription is included and the mirrors were given to her as a gift. No mention is made of the inscription's meaning, so I assume she doesn't know.

There are other curious instructions that mandate that your mirror must only be framed on three sides; the left side being unframed and open.

The mirror is used as a means of discovering the identity of an individual; in particular a witch who is *verhexing* either you or your client. The instructions are to engrave the barbarous words on the back of the mirror, then hide/bury it in a crossroads three nights before the dark of the moon. Keep it hidden there for three days. On the third day, return to the mirror at midnight and take it out of hiding. Make sure you block all light by covering your head with a black cloth and not allowing any light to hit the mirror's surface. There is to be total silence while you use the mirror. Cover your head and the mirror and look at the mirror and you will see the face of the witch. It is also stated that you should take your dog or cat with you so that they are the first to look in the mirror before you do. No harm befalls the animal, apparently.

When not in use, your mirror should be kept wrapped in black cloth and hidden away in a secret location. When you need it again, you must bury/hide it for three days just as you did the first time.

Weather Prediction

This section is a tribute to some of the quaint beliefs and superstitions of the Pennsylvania Germans. Although not technically a part of the tradition of Powwow, these curious beliefs about prediction the weather can still have merit, should you choose to learn them. I have a million such signs and weather portents, but I am sharing here some of the most common and useful for your enjoyment.

For snow: predicting snow and frost is a very big deal in Pennsylvania; especially if you are a farmer or gardener. Once October comes, we are on the lookout for the first snow fall. Our pets give us our fist clues. If your dog howls at the moon, expect the first snow fall soon. If your cat sits with her back to the fireplace, snow is on its way.

Frost requires a little tricky calendar work. Once the katydids start singing, count 90 days. That's when the first frost hits. Count the number of mornings in August when fog covers the ground. That's how many snowfalls we will have come winter.

Keep your eye on the first 12 days of the year. Each of those days represent the weather of each of the coming 12 months.

When the smoke stops rising up the chimney and instead fills up the house, snow is on its way.

A ring around the moon indicates snow in the next three days. Two rings and it means snow in the next 24 hours.

For rain: when the cows lay down in the fields during the day, rain is coming.

When your cat lays on its head, rain will follow.

When your dog starts eating grass, it means rain is in the air.

When the leaves show their backsides, a storm is approaching.

Northern winds signify cold and windy days.

Eastern winds signify powerful storms; even tornadoes.

Southern winds can mean lots of rain, but sometimes can be warm and pleasant.

Western winds are most favorable.

In the evening when the sky is red, the next day will be fair. In the morning, a red sky indicates storms.

The Moon: many of the old farmers believe the phase or appearance of the moon gives an indication of the weather to come.

Horns pointing up, rain within three days.

Horns pointing down signifies a dry spell.

A full moon obscured by clouds brings sunshine and dry weather.

Chapter Eight

The other side of Powwow

Ceremonial Magic

Welcome to another side of Powwow that most people have never seen before; the ceremonial magic aspect of the tradition. There is debate as to whether or not Powwows ever engaged in such things. I myself have not come across much in the way of research to indicate that Powwowers of old engaged in these types of practices. However, ceremonial magic is, in my opinion, a natural progression for the Powwow if he or she feels inclined to take their practice to the next level.

The ceremonial magic practices that follow have been pieced together by me using the various Grimoires and source materials for Powwowing, as well as biblical sources and Judeo-Christian ritualized ceremonial magic sources.

Everything has been pieced together with the utmost respect for the cultural, historical, and traditional considerations of

Powwow. If the reader feels there are mistakes in the ceremonial rites included here, those mistakes are entirely my own and should not reflect on the tradition of Powwowing itself because, as stated, these additions to the tradition are of my own design.

In the first section I will introduce you to astrological correspondences, which we know for a fact are utilized by the Pennsylvania Germans in their farming and harvesting almanacs. The various Powwow Grimoires available to us from history show dates considered both favorable and unfavorable for various conditions. The information I have included here is only an expansion on that material and does not detract from what the Pennsylvania Germans already know about astrological influences.

We also know for a fact that Powwowers made talismans and amulets, as is evident by the *himmelsbriefs*, which were hand-written talismans, and *anhangsel*, which were astrological amulets.

Prayers and invocations to angels and archangels would have been largely foreign to the Reformed and Lutheran within the community, but not the Catholics. John George Hohman, author of *Long Lost Friend*, was a Catholic. He would have been quite familiar and comfortable with the idea of angels and archangels playing a role in healing and protection work.

The only other elements that I've added come to us from the *Lesser Key of Solomon*, a Grimoire that utilizes Judeo-Christian symbolism. The creation of the magic circle comes almost word-for-word from *Key of Solomon* and utilizes nothing more than a select handful of verses from the *Book of Psalms*. There is nothing unfamiliar about the Old Testament to the Pennsylvania Germans, most especially amongst the Anabaptists.

Finally, my inclusion of the Lesser Banishing Ritual of the Pentagram can rightfully and honestly be considered the only addition that doesn't truly fit. There isn't a single shred of research or evidence (that I have found) to show that any Powwow or Pennsylvania German utilized the Lesser Banishing Ritual in any form. However, once you see the other ceremonial elements I've put together, you will (hopefully) understand why I believe the LBR

is a perfect accompaniment.

Read through this section with an open mind. There is

nothing here that is spooky or strange. This is Christian magic at its

most elaborate and involved. The ritualistic elements here are not

for the dabbler or the simple folk healer. This is another level of

Powwowing that speaks directly to the unwavering faith required in

order to successfully work magic and the desire to experience God

firsthand, rather than as a mere spectator at a Sunday morning

service.

If your goal is to fully immerse yourself into the experience

of being a Hex Doctor, a true master of all aspects of the Powwow

tradition, then read on.

Sun Mercury Venus Earth

Moon Mars Ceres Jupiter

Saturn Uranus Neptune Pluto

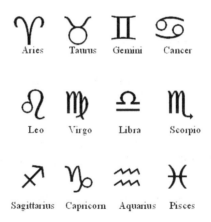

Aries Taurus Gemini Cancer

Leo Virgo Libra Scorpio

Sagittarius Capricorn Aquarius Pisces

125

The virtues of the planets and signs of the zodiac

Astrology is an extremely complex study. Years ago, I took a 12 week astrology course which taught the basics of interpreting natal and transit charts and touched briefly on predictive astrological techniques. I found the class to be fascinating and, it turned out, I had a natural aptitude for the subject. From that moment on, I was hooked. Astrology has been a part of my folk magic practice since then and I've expanded greatly on my knowledge through study and input from others better schooled in the discipline than I am.

Because of its complexity, astrology can seem daunting to some, which is likely why it isn't so popular these days. For the purpose of Powwowing, your astrological understanding should be at least entry-level; meaning you could benefit greatly just by understanding the influence of each sign and how those influences come into play as the sun and moon pass through those signs. For the practitioner of magic, astrology will help add depth and power to the work you are planning. I've kept the information to a minimum; providing just as much as you'll need to get by. Should you wish to go further with your studies of this amazing subject, there are nearly countless resources available to you online.

What follows here is a basic introduction to the energy of the planets and the signs as they are known to the Pennsylvania Germans. As well as some planting and harvesting advice that will prove useful to those of us who garden or farm. In addition, some lunar information will round out the introduction to this element of the magical operation.

This section will focus specifically on the energies of each planet and sign and how to utilize those energies; either with the creation of talismans or with the calculation of planetary hours. Don't be discouraged, it's not as technical or difficult as it sounds.

In the Christian worldview, the planets and signs are understood to have been created by God and are under the command of God. They are not gods themselves, but rather powers and principles under the authority of the Almighty, such as with angels and archangels, but more on this later. As such, the planets can be petitioned as reserves of energy to effect specific and certain functions. The signs are fixed points in the sky that influence the energy of the planets as they pass through them. Think of the planets as different people and the signs as different situations those people find themselves in. That's not exactly how it works, but it's a good start.

Let's start with the signs, their planetary rulers, and their general energies.

Aries. The Ram. Rules the head. First of the signs of the zodiac. Cardinal fire sign. Aries is governed by the planet Mars. Seeds planted in this sign produce vines or stalks. All crops that produce their yield above the surface of the ground should be planted in the new or increase light of the moon to grow vigorously. For best yield, grain should be planted in the dark of the moon. The important points of Aries are energy, activity, and leadership.

Taurus. The Bull. Rules the throat and neck. Fixed earth sign governed by Venus. Will do well for all root crops of quick growth. All root crops that produce their yield in the ground should be planted during the old or decrease light of the moon to produce a good yield. Key points of Taurus are endurance, persistence, and sensuality.

Gemini. The Twins. Rules the arms, lungs, and hands. Third sign of the zodiac. Ruled by Mercury. Barren sign. Good for planting melon seeds. A good sign to stir the soil to subdue all noxious weeds. Plants that produce their yield above the ground may be planted in any sign of the upper part of the body. Important words for Gemini are versatility and ingenuity.

Cancer. The Crab. Rules the breast. Cardinal sign. A watery fruitful movable sign. Germinate quickly. It is favorable to growth and insures an abundant yield. If it comes at full of the moon it is a good time to plant beans. If at time of new moon, lentils. Best time to sow peas if the day follows the new moon, as they will grow quickly, have abundant flowers and yield; peas, if sown immediately after the second quarter, will bear but little; if sown a day or two after the full moon will bloom and fruit in abundance, but no yield. If the sign comes just before the full of the moon it is a good time to plant or purse fruit trees. Cancer is a good sign to prune grape vines. Keywords for Cancer are sensitivity, the home, sympathy, affection, and family.

Leo. The Lion. Rules the heart. A barren fixed fire sign; is only favorable to the destruction of noxious growth. Weeds, briars, and bushes cut off in the old of the moon in August when its place is in Leo will be more certainly destroyed than if done at any other time. The timber cut in the old of the moon in August will not be eaten by worms nor snap in burning, and will last much longer than if cut at any other time. Important words for Leo are vitality, confidence, self-expression, and leadership.

Virgo. The Virgin. Rules the bowels/intestines. A mutable earth sign. A barren sign. Ruled by Mercury. Makes many and beautiful flowers, but unfavorable to the growth of seed or transplanting. The keywords for Virgo are efficiency, discernment, and service.

Libra. The Scales. Rules the reins/kidneys. A strong cardinal air sign. Ruled by the planet Venus. Seed planted at this time produce vigorous pulp growth and roots and a reasonable amount of grain. Important points of Libra are balance, diplomacy, and relations with others.

Scorpio. The Scorpion. Rules the loins. Ruled by the planet Pluto, which is a higher octave of Mars. A fruitful sign producing watery effects. A fixed sign. A good sign to plant corn. Keywords for Scorpio are secrecy, regeneration, and power.

Sagittarius. The Archer. Rules the thighs and hips. Fiery mutable masculine sign. Ruled by Jupiter. Will not do well as it is not a very favorable time to plant or transplant. If the moon is dark or on the wane, radishes or potatoes may be planted, as root crops are said to do well if planted in signs of lower parts of the body. Keywords for Sagittarius are honesty, exploration, and idealism.

Capricorn. The Goat. Rules the knees. Ruled by Saturn. A cardinal earth sign. Produces rapid growth of pulp stalk or roots, but not much grain. Important points of Capricorn are ambition, diligence, and perseverance.

Aquarius. The Water Bearer., Rules the legs. Airy masculine sign. Ruled by Uranus, which is a higher octave of Mercury. Seed does not grow well. Do not plant seed as it will rot, and is only thrown away. Keywords are detachment, humanitarianism, and independence.

Pisces. The Fish. Rules the feet. A watery feminine sign; will produce excellent results and is one of the best signs for producing the fruit

The Powwow Grimoire

S	A	T	O	R
A	R	E	P	O
T	E	N	E	T
O	P	E	R	A
R	O	T	A	S

of the earth. Ruled by Neptune, a higher octave of Venus. Being a watery sign assists vegetation to withstand a drought. This is an especially good sign if the moon is dark or on the wane. This is a good sing to make sauerkraut. Keywords are compassion, receptivity, and imagination.

Now, what to do with all of that information? Each part of the body is ruled by a sign of the zodiac. Imagine someone comes to you for healing a specific area of their body. Using the astrological information you have here, you know that it would be favorable to your work if the sun or moon was passing through that particular zodiac sign that correlates to the area of the body that you are asked to heal. The same holds true for planting/harvesting. Use the information above to determine when the best time is for planting/harvesting certain crops.

The sun passes through each sign once a year and stays in each sign for about 28 days, give or take. This is how we get our 12 zodiac times of the year.

The moon passes through each sign once a month and stays in that sign for approximately 2 to 2 1/2 days, give or take.

Each day of the week also has a sign/planet ruler. So, if you can't wait for the right time of year, and you can't wait for the right day in a month, you can hold out for the best day of that particular week.

To further fine tune things, and especially if you can't wait for the sun or moon to get into that particular sign and can't even wait for another day in your current week, you have what is known as planetary hours. Planetary hours are sections of each day and night that are ruled by each sign of the zodiac.

Planetary Hours

The idea behind Planetary hours is that the entire day from sunrise to sunset is divided into twelve equal segments. These are known as Planetary hours, although they may not actually be an hour long.

Step 1: Check your local almanac or weather station for exact sunrise and sunset times for your day.

Ex. Sunrise 6:14am - Sunset 6:30pm

Step 2: translate that time into minutes.

Ex. 6:14am to 6:30pm is 736 minutes.

Step 3: divide those minutes into 12.

Ex. 12/736 = 61. Each of your planetary hours is 61 minutes long

Step 4: these 12 hours from sunrise to sunset are known as Sunrise Planetary Hours. Your next step is to calculate the 12 planetary hours from sunset to sunrise the next morning. These are your Sunset Planetary Hours.

Step 5: find sunset time to sunrise the next morning

Ex. 6:30pm to 6:01am = 631 minutes. 12/691 = 57.5 round up to 58. Each of your Sunset Planetary Hours is 58 minutes long.

Now look at the following chart that outlines each day, sign, planet, part of body, and metal. This metal information will be useful when we discuss talismans later on.

Day	Sign	Planet	Body part	Metal
Sunday	Leo	Sun	Heart	Gold
Monday	Cancer	Moon	Breast	Silver
Tuesday	Aries, Scorpio	Mars	Head and face, loins	Iron
Wednesday	Gemini, Virgo	Mercury	shoulders, bowels	Mercury
Thursday	Sagittarius, Pisces	Jupiter	Thighs, feet	Tin
Friday	Taurus, Libra	Venus	Neck, forearms	Copper
Saturday	Capricorn, Aquarius	Saturn	Knees, bones, teeth, legs	Lead

Using the chart on the previous page that shows the planetary ruler of each day, we can easily place our planetary hours into the twelve equal segments that we calculated earlier.

Ex. On Monday, the sunrise and sunset times are 6:14am to 6:30pm. Using our calculations, the planetary hours are 61 minutes long. Because it's Monday, the planetary ruler of the day is the Moon. So, we begin noting down what times of day are ruled by each planet using this order:

Moon, Saturn, Jupiter, Mars, Sun, Venus, Mercury and repeat from the beginning until all of your hours are assigned a planetary ruler.

Each day, as shown in the previous chart, has a planetary ruler. On that day, you will begin your list of planetary hours with that day's ruler, as shown here:

Sunday

Sun, Venus, Mercury, Moon, Saturn, Jupiter, Mars

Monday

Moon, Saturn, Jupiter, Mars, Sun, Venus, Mercury

Tuesday

Mars, Sun, Venus, Mercury, Moon, Saturn, Jupiter

Wednesday

Mercury, Moon, Saturn, Jupiter, Mars, Sun, Venus

Thursday

Jupiter, Mars, Sun, Venus, Mercury, Moon, Saturn

Friday

Venus, Mercury, Moon, Saturn, Jupiter, Mars, Sun

Saturday

Saturn, Jupiter, Mars, Sun, Venus, Mercury, Moon

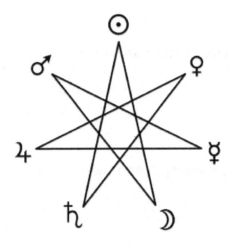

The Heptagram. Begin at the symbol for your chosen day (refer to symbol chart on page 125) then follow the symbols clockwise around the circle for your planetary hours.

Don't be overwhelmed by all of this. It's not essential to your powwowing work. It just adds an extra depth. Planetary hours fine tune your work and are especially empowering when you are creating talismans, which we will get to in the next section. Keep all of the charts and images from this section handy, as you will refer

to them often when creating talismans.

Talismans

The creation of talismans need not be complex. If you understand the astrological information presented in the previous section, then talismans should be fairly simple to understand.

The purpose of a talisman is to attract a specific influence into the bearer's life. This could be strength, protection, luck, prosperity, love, abundance, or any other influence or thing the individual wishes to attract. Talismans bring something toward you.

Planetary talismans are made under very specific planetary influences and conditions. First, the creator of the talisman will ascertain the exact desire of the individual. Then he will determine under which sign to create the talisman. Use the chart on the next page to help determine which planetary influence best matches your goal. Blend this information with the chart on page 125 to help determine the best day of the week and planetary hour in which to create your talisman. You will also choose the best metal to construct your talisman using the chart on page 125.

A quick note here about access to metals. This can be extremely tricky, especially if your funds are rather limited. I have found that working with a metal that is the correct color can be sufficient. You can find thin sheets of workable aluminum in various colors at craft shops. If you truly want the talisman to be properly empowered, however, then it is well worth your effort and cash to track down the appropriate metals.

Planet	General Influences
Sun	Fortune, riches, success, happiness, victory, fatherhood
Moon	Family, secrets, dreams, motherhood, children, the home
Mars	Triumph, battle, protection, sex, assertiveness, confidence

Mercury	Communication, discussion, interviews, talent, travel
Jupiter	Expansion, success, travel, education, teachers, open-mindedness
Venus	Love, beauty, self-improvement, money, relationships, talents
Saturn	Control, regulations, rules, banishing, binding, authority

Before we start creating talismans, let's cover one more area that will help fine tune the work you are doing: the phase of the moon.

The phases of the moon are important to planting and harvesting and they are equally important to the creation of talismans.

Generally speaking, the moon's energies ebb and flow with its phases. The New Moon (often called the Dark Moon) is when the moon is not visible in the sky. From this point to approximately 7 days later, the moon is in its First Quarter. This is a time of building and beginnings and powwowing for the increase of something is empowered at this time.

From 7 to 14 days after the New Moon the moon is in its Second Quarter. It culminates in a Full Moon. This phase of the moon is for empowering your healing, increasing something, building something, etc.

From the Full Moon to 7 days after is the Third Quarter. This is a time of decrease; a time of things fading and going away. Hex removal and protection charms are empowered at this time.

From 7 to 14 days after the Full Moon is the Last Quarter. This is a time of banishing, binding, curse removal, combating witchcraft and elimination.

The moon travels through each of the Zodiac signs every 28 days. It stays in a sign for approximately 2.5 days (give or take). During those times, conditions for the parts of the body ruled by that sign are more favorable. Remember: when in need, do the powwowing. Don't wait for proper moon phase or sign. Do what you need to do, when you need to do it. However, the moon's energies can add something extra to your work, so if it's possible to wait, then do so.

For creating talismans, I personally feel it's important to wait for the appropriate moon phase, in addition to the best day, best planetary hour, etc. The more you can fine tune your work, the more effective your talisman will be.

A talisman is created by first cutting a round disk from the metal you are working with. On one side of the disk you will engrave a five pointed star, called a pentagram.

On the opposite side of the disk you will engrave a six pointed star, called a hexagram.

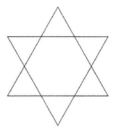

On the pentagram side of the disk you will engrave symbols and writing to specify the goal of the talisman. This could include a sword image for protection or a heart for love or a coin for prosperity and so on. You are only limited by your engraving skills and the size of the talisman. Generally, the symbol is placed in the center of the pentagram.

Around the edges of the pentagram will be letters and words describing your desire. Keep this simple as you will have limited space to work with. For example, for a talisman for protection, stick to the word "protection" or "safety". The words are engraved using what is known as the Alphabet of the Magi (see next page).

Alphabet of the Magi

The Alphabet of the Magi

On the opposite side of the talisman, the hexagram is used to honor God and ask for His blessing on the power of the talisman. In the center of the hexagram you can engrave an image that represents God or an offering you are making to Him. Knowledge of the Bible helps here because the images can represent themes from various stories in the Bible. For example, an image of a whip can be drawn to ask God's favor in overcoming those who seek to steal from you (remember that time Jesus whipped the business men in the temple?). Or you can choose an image of an angel if your talisman is designed to bring you a message of some sort. You must use your creativity with this.

Around the edges of the hexagram, using the Alphabet of the Magi, you will write words praising God and thanking Him for bringing the desire to manifest. Keep it short, as space is limited.

Remember that you will be crafting the talisman during the correct planetary hour, on the correct day, under the correct zodiac sign if possible (whether the moon or sun is in the sign). Consult an almanac to find the exact zodiac position of the sun or moon.

What follows are examples of planetary talismans from the old Grimoires. I've included them here so that you can see what a finished talisman will look like (although the images and words should be specific for your or your client's needs).

Obverse   Talisman of the Moon   Reverse

Obverse   Reverse

Talisman of Mars

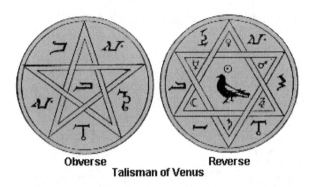

Obverse   Reverse

Talisman of Venus

Obverse   Reverse

Talisman of the Sun

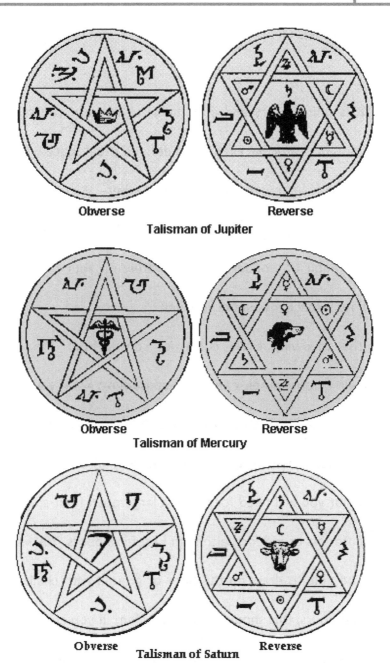

Obverse   Reverse

Talisman of Jupiter

Obverse   Reverse

Talisman of Mercury

Obverse   Reverse

Talisman of Saturn

The Powwow Grimoire

S A T O R
A R E P O
T E N E T
O P E R A
R O T A S

The Magic Circle

It is unnecessary and impractical to concern yourself with the creation of protective circles and defined ritual space when you are faced with an emergency situation where your Powwowing skills are needed. However, if you entertain clients in your home or are in the habit of working magic privately on your own, then a defined ritual space may serve you well.

The following circle construct comes from *The Key of Solomon*. It is both complex and time consuming. Yet if you were to compare it to the instructions within that old Grimoire, you will find that my version is actually quite simple in comparison.

What you will need for this is a large open floor space. This can be outdoors or indoors, although I prefer indoors. You will also need to be able to draw on the floor or ground with chalk. If you have wood floors, this shouldn't be a problem. If you are outside in the dirt, then I suggest scratching the markings in the dirt with a stick.

Your circle space should be 6' across so that you have plenty of space to move about. If you can do a larger space, then I suggest 9' across. If you want your circle to be as perfect as you can draw it, I suggest planting something heavy in the center of your space and tying a string to it that is at least 3' long or, if you have a larger space, then 4' 6". This will give you a circle 6' across and 9' across respectively.

You will also need your Bible. *The Key of Solomon* refers to the King James Version. If you have a more modern version that you prefer, I see no issue with this at all. You will be working from Psalms.

To begin, stand in the center of your ritual area and face East. You are going to be reading Psalm 2 from the Bible. I've included it here. Psalm 2 is a declaration that, despite the evils of the world, you remain devoted to God.

1 Why do the heathen rage, and the people imagine a vain thing?

2 The kings of the earth set themselves, and the rulers take counsel together, against the LORD, and against his anointed, saying,

3 Let us break their bands asunder, and cast away their cords from us.

4 He that sitteth in the heavens shall laugh: the Lord shall have them in derision.

5 Then shall he speak unto them in his wrath, and vex them in his sore displeasure.

6 Yet have I set my king upon my holy hill of Zion.

7 I will declare the decree: the LORD hath said unto me, Thou art my Son; this day have I begotten thee.

8 Ask of me, and I shall give thee the heathen for thine inheritance, and the uttermost parts of the earth for thy possession.

9 Thou shalt break them with a rod of iron; thou shalt dash them in pieces like a potter's vessel.

10 Be wise now therefore, O ye kings: be instructed, ye judges of the earth.

11 Serve the LORD with fear, and rejoice with trembling.

12 Kiss the Son, lest he be angry, and ye perish from the way, when his wrath is kindled but a little. Blessed are all they that put their trust in him.

Once finished reciting Psalm 2, draw out your magic circle on the ground or floor, as shown below.

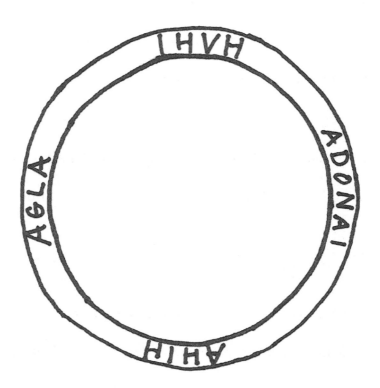

The intonations for the names of God are written in between the two drawn circles.

IHVH (in the East) is the unknowable name of God. It is pronounced *ye-ho-wah*.

ADONAI (in the South) translates as LORD. It is pronounced *ah-doh-nie*.

AHIH (in the West) translates as I AM. It is pronounced *eh-aye-ah*.

AGLA (in the North) is the abbreviated intonation for "Thou are might forever, my Lord." It is pronounced *ag-lah*.

For the next step, you will be reciting Psalm 53. For this, you will face West and kneel on the floor/ground. This Psalm is not only a dedication of your faith, but a lament on those who deny the existence of God.

1 The fool hath said in his heart, There is no God. Corrupt are they, and have done abominable iniquity: there is none that doeth good.

2 God looked down from heaven upon the children of men, to see if there were any that did understand, that did seek God.

3 Every one of them is gone back: they are altogether become filthy; there is none that doeth good, no, not one.

4 Have the workers of iniquity no knowledge? who eat up my people as they eat bread: they have not called upon God.

5 There were they in great fear, where no fear was: for God hath scattered the bones of him that encampeth against thee: thou hast put them to shame, because God hath despised them.

6 Oh that the salvation of Israel were come out of Zion! When God bringeth back the captivity of his people, Jacob shall rejoice, and Israel shall be glad.

When you are finished reciting this Psalm, offer a moment of silent prayer and reflection and give a silent prayer of thanks for your faith.

For the next step in the construction of your magic circle, you will stand and move back to the East. As you recite Psalm 112, you will be moving around the circle in a clockwise direction. This is a much more upbeat and positive declaration of the Powwower's recognition of God's power and love. The word "righteous" is a word fraught with negative connotations, simply because we are all aware of the arrogance of self-righteousness. However, to be "righteous" in the Biblical sense is to be right with God. Metaphysically speaking, this also means to be right within yourself. In other words, we must strive for purity of self in order to effectively help others. Psalm 112 affirms this.

1 Praise ye the LORD. Blessed is the man that feareth the LORD, that delighteth greatly in his commandments.

2 His seed shall be mighty upon earth: the generation of the upright shall be blessed.

3 Wealth and riches shall be in his house: and his righteousness endureth for ever.

4 Unto the upright there ariseth light in the darkness: he is gracious, and full of compassion, and righteous.

5 A good man sheweth favour, and lendeth: he will guide his affairs with discretion.

6 Surely he shall not be moved for ever: the righteous shall be in everlasting remembrance.

7 He shall not be afraid of evil tidings: his heart is fixed, trusting in the LORD.

8 His heart is established, he shall not be afraid, until he see his desire upon his enemies.

9 He hath dispersed, he hath given to the poor; his righteousness endureth for ever; his horn shall be exalted with honour.

10 The wicked shall see it, and be grieved; he shall gnash with his teeth, and melt away: the desire of the wicked shall perish.

Psalm 66 represent supplications before God and praising Him for both the good and the bad that has come upon you in life.

It is an experience of humbling, which puts us in a proper frame of mind for experiencing the awesome power of the Creator. I believe that awe and respect for spiritual power is key to effective magic.

For this part of the circle construction, you should be standing and facing East. Your circle is mostly complete and now is the time to praise God and recognize the awesome power you will be working with.

1 Make a joyful noise unto God, all ye lands:

2 Sing forth the honour of his name: make his praise glorious.

3 Say unto God, How terrible art thou in thy works! through the greatness of thy power shall thine enemies submit themselves unto thee.

4 All the earth shall worship thee, and shall sing unto thee; they shall sing to thy name. Selah.

5 Come and see the works of God: he is terrible in his doing toward the children of men.

6 He turned the sea into dry land: they went through the flood on foot: there did we rejoice in him.

7 He ruleth by his power for ever; his eyes behold the nations: let not the rebellious exalt themselves. Selah.

8 O bless our God, ye people, and make the voice of his praise to be heard:

9 Which holdeth our soul in life, and suffereth not our feet to be moved.

10 For thou, O God, hast proved us: thou hast tried us, as silver is tried.

11 Thou broughtest us into the net; thou laidst affliction upon our loins.

12 Thou hast caused men to ride over our heads; we went through fire and through water: but thou broughtest us out into a wealthy place.

13 I will go into thy house with burnt offerings: I will pay thee my vows,

14 Which my lips have uttered, and my mouth hath spoken, when I was in trouble.

15 I will offer unto thee burnt sacrifices of fatlings, with the incense of rams; I will offer bullocks with goats. Selah.

16 Come and hear, all ye that fear God, and I will declare what he hath done for my soul.

17 I cried unto him with my mouth, and he was extolled with my tongue.

18 If I regard iniquity in my heart, the Lord will not hear me:

19 But verily God hath heard me; he hath attended to the voice of my prayer.

20 Blessed be God, which hath not turned away my prayer, nor his mercy from me.

Psalm 46 finalizes the power of the magic circle and locks it in place as a protective mechanism in which to do your work. With the recitation of this Psalm you are stating that you are safe and protected by God, which renders any ill influences powerless against you.

1 God is our refuge and strength, a very present help in trouble.

2 Therefore will not we fear, though the earth be removed, and though the mountains be carried into the midst of the sea;

3 Though the waters thereof roar and be troubled, though the mountains shake with the swelling thereof. Selah.

4 There is a river, the streams whereof shall make glad the city of God, the holy place of the tabernacles of the most High.

5 God is in the midst of her; she shall not be moved: God shall help her, and that right early.

6 The heathen raged, the kingdoms were moved: he uttered his voice, the earth melted.

7 The LORD of hosts is with us; the God of Jacob is our refuge. Selah.

8 Come, behold the works of the LORD, what desolations he hath made in the earth.

9 He maketh wars to cease unto the end of the earth; he breaketh the bow, and cutteth the spear in sunder; he burneth the chariot in the fire.

10 Be still, and know that I am God: I will be exalted among the heathen, I will be exalted in the earth.

11 The LORD of hosts is with us; the God of Jacob is our refuge. Selah.

Psalm 67 is the invocation to God to take part in your work. As always with speaking to God, there is to be a balance of praise and supplication.

1 God be merciful unto us, and bless us; and cause his face to shine upon us; Selah.

2 That thy way may be known upon earth, thy saving health among all nations.

3 Let the people praise thee, O God; let all the people praise thee.

4 O let the nations be glad and sing for joy: for thou shalt judge the people righteously, and govern the nations upon earth. Selah.

5 Let the people praise thee, O God; let all the people praise thee.

6 Then shall the earth yield her increase; and God, even our own God, shall bless us.

7 God shall bless us; and all the ends of the earth shall fear him.

And lastly, Psalm 50 is God's promise to answer those who call on Him in faith and devotion. I also see within Psalm 50 a reminder to those who would deny His existence, yet twist holy writings and ritual for their own ego-gratification that God cannot be deceived.

The mighty God, even the LORD, hath spoken, and called the earth from the rising of the sun unto the going down thereof.

2 Out of Zion, the perfection of beauty, God hath shined.

3 Our God shall come, and shall not keep silence: a fire shall devour before him, and it shall be very tempestuous round about him.

4 He shall call to the heavens from above, and to the earth, that he may judge his people.

5 Gather my saints together unto me; those that have made a covenant with me by sacrifice.

6 And the heavens shall declare his righteousness: for God is judge himself. Selah.

7 Hear, O my people, and I will speak; O Israel, and I will testify against thee: I am God, even thy God.

8 I will not reprove thee for thy sacrifices or thy burnt offerings, to have been continually before me.

9 I will take no bullock out of thy house, nor he goats out of thy folds.

10 For every beast of the forest is mine, and the cattle upon a thousand hills.

11 I know all the fowls of the mountains: and the wild beasts of the field are mine.

12 If I were hungry, I would not tell thee: for the world is mine, and the fullness thereof.

13 Will I eat the flesh of bulls, or drink the blood of goats?

14 Offer unto God thanksgiving; and pay thy vows unto the most High:

15 And call upon me in the day of trouble: I will deliver thee, and thou shalt glorify me.

16 But unto the wicked God saith, What hast thou to do to declare my statutes, or that thou shouldest take my covenant in thy mouth?

17 Seeing thou hatest instruction, and castest my words behind thee.

18 When thou sawest a thief, then thou consentedst with him, and hast been partaker with adulterers.

19 Thou givest thy mouth to evil, and thy tongue frameth deceit.

20 Thou sittest and speakest against thy brother; thou slanderest thine own mother's son.

21 These things hast thou done, and I kept silence; thou thoughtest that I was altogether such an one as thyself: but I will reprove thee, and set them in order before thine eyes.

22 Now consider this, ye that forget God, lest I tear you in pieces, and there be none to deliver.

23 Whoso offereth praise glorifieth me: and to him that ordereth his conversation aright will I shew the salvation of God.

Reading through these Psalms within your magic circle and preparing for magical work is an extremely powerful experience, I promise you. When your faith is strong and your connection to God is secure, your magic will be far more powerful than you can imagine.

Over the years I have had MANY people complain to me that Powwow is "too Christian" or "too religious" and that my ceremonial additions are "too preachy". I make no apologies for this. Powwow is what it is. Ceremonial magic is what it is. If you don't like it or if you lack the faith to perform this type of work, my advice would be to find something else better suited to you. Powwow requires actual faith in God. The ceremonial magic elements that I utilize require you to actually feel awe in the face of the divine. You can't fake your way through it.

Once your magic circle is complete, it's time to make your talismans. You can take your time with this, but do try to plan at least the beginning of your work with the proper planetary hour. Make sure you do not leave your circle for any reason during your work. Remain within until the talisman is complete. All the while you should be asking God for His assistance in empowering the talisman to serve its intended purpose.

When you are finished, it's time to close things up. The method I have chosen for closing things down is the Lesser Banishing Ritual of the Pentagram. This rite fits perfectly into the ceremonial elements of Powwowing and works best for clearing away all the energies you've accumulated during your talismanic work.

You need not limit yourself to just talismanic work within the circle. If you are doing distance Powwowing for someone, you may choose to do such work within the safety of the magic circle. You can create himmelsbriefs within the circle, if you wish. You can also just create the magic circle if you feel you need a little protection for yourself. There are no hard and fast rules about usage for the magic circle.

When you are finished with your work, clean up your tools and supplies. Place everything at the edge of the circle so that it is all out of your way. Now you will clear away the circle using the Lesser Banishing Ritual.

The Powwow Grimoire

S	A	T	O	R
A	R	E	P	O
T	E	N	E	T
O	P	E	R	A
R	O	T	A	S

The Lesser Banishing Ritual

This rite is designed to banish any and all energies; good, bad, or otherwise. The LBR invokes the divine within you as well as without. It is perfect for clearing away your space after ritual.

Here is the Lesser Banishing Ritual as I use it. Note that there are many variations to the LBR, with additional rites used by some practitioners. Again, this is not a traditional aspect to Powwowing but, as you will see, it fits perfectly into the ceremonial elements that I have added to my personal practice.

Facing East, assume a prayerful attitude. Touch your forehead and intone **ATEH** (ah-tay) which translates as "For thine is"

Touch your chest and intone **MALKUTH** (mal-kooth) which translates as "the Kingdom".

Touch your right shoulder and intone **VEGEBURAH** (vay-gay-boo-rah) which translates as "and the Power".

Touch your left shoulder and intone **VEGEDULAH** (vay-gay-doo-lah) which translates as "and the Glory".

Clasp your hands upon your chest and intone **LE-OLAHM, AMEN** (lay-oh-lahm, ah-men) which translates as "Forever, Amen".

Facing East, visualize a pentagram of blue flame in the air before you and intone **IHVH** (ye-ho-way) which is the unknowable name of God.

Facing South, visualize a pentagram of blue flame in the air before you and intone **ADONAI** (ah-do-nie) which translates as LORD.

Facing West, visualize a pentagram of blue flame in the air before you and intone **AHIH** (ey-aye-ah) which translates as I AM.

Facing North, visualize a pentagram of blue flame in the air before you and intone **AGLA** (ag-lah) which is the abbreviated intonation for "Thou art might and forever, my Lord."

Turn back to facing East. Extend both arms outward to form your body into a cross and say, *"Before me, Raphael* (intone the name like Rah-Phy-Ell). *Behind me, Gabriel* (Gah-bree-ell). *On my right, Michael* (Mee-kay-ell). *On my left, Auriel* (Aur-ee-ell). *Around me flames the pentagrams. Above me shines the six-rayed star."* Envision a blue flamed hexagram above you.

Now allow yourself a moment to envision the pentagrams around you and the hexagram above you. Feel the power and glory of God surrounding and permeating you. Allow the visuals and feeling to fade naturally. When you feel you are finished, open your eyes. The rite is complete. The magic circle is cleared away. Clean up your belongings, wipe away all traces of your circle, then go about your normal daily business.

The Angels

In the original editions of this Grimoire, I included information on angels and archangels that could be called upon to aid in the creation of talismans. I have chosen to reduce some of this information as I felt that some of it was unnecessary for the proper practice of the ceremonial elements and it was a bit irresponsible of me to include information that may take the practitioner into different realms of magic outside the practice of Powwowing. Therefore, I will allow other authors of various ceremonial traditions to elaborate further on angelic/archangelic work. For the purposes of the ceremonial elements to Powwowing, I will stick with descriptions for just those invoked during the Lesser Banishing Ritual; Raphael, Gabriel, Michael, and Auriel.

Raphael

Raphael's name means "God has healed". His name comes from the Hebrew rapha, meaning "healer" or "doctor". Raphael is attributed with many healings and the sharing of medical wisdom with humans. In some ways, Raphael could be a patron for Powwowing, as the healing arts are his realm. The ring that King Solomon bore to protect from demons was allegedly given to him by Raphael. The symbol on that ring was the hexagram.

Gabriel

Gabriel's name means "God is my strength". Gabriel is described as having 140 pairs of wings and is the guardian of Eden. Gabriel is alternatively depicted as both male and female. Gabriel is the angel of mercy, death, revelation, vengeance, the Resurrection, and the Annunciation. Gabriel appears to Daniel to tell him of the eventual coming of the Messiah. 500 years later, Gabriel appears to Mary with the same message. Gabriel is the chief ambassador of God to humanity.

Michael

Michael is often considered to be the greatest of all of God's angels. His name translates as "he who is like God". It is Michael who, at the end of days, will come down from heaven with the keys to the abyss and the chains which will bind the Devil for a thousand years. Michael is generally depicted as wearing armor and carrying an unsheathed sword. He is almost always seen standing triumphant atop the vanquished Devil. Michael is referred to as the "Prince of Light" in the Dead Sea Scrolls.

Auriel

Auriel's name means "God is my light". He is the angel of glory and sanctification. In the Book of Enoch, Auriel, along with Raphael, Gabriel, and Michael, are known as the "Watchers"; angels who are given instruction to watch over and protect mankind. Auriel is sometimes seen spelled Uriel, but the two are one and the same.

Chapter Nine

Conclusion

Pennsylvania is an extremely interesting and unique state, and that is in no small part due to the diversity of our religious history. When William Penn sent out his invitations welcoming those who desired freedom of religion to come to Pennsylvania, he had a dream of creating a haven for all those who believed in God to come here and make a home for themselves and worship God as they saw fit. This opened the way for a number of different traditions to establish homes and lives here in the Commonwealth.

"All men have a natural and indefeasible right to worship Almighty God according to the dictates of their own consciences; no man can of right be compelled to attend, erect, or support any place of worship...against his consent."

William Penn, Declaration of Rights, 1682

Today, the Pennsylvania landscape, both physical and religious, has scarcely changed from those early days. No matter how many cities and housing developments we build or how many churches we erect, we are still the state of religious tolerance and freedom. It is no surprise that such a diverse culture would nurture a tradition such as Powwowing.

I hope I have achieved my goal of offering a thorough explanation of the practices of the Powwow Doctor. There is much more I could have included here, but my goal of offering a workable and usable Grimoire for the would-be practitioner is, I feel, accomplished.

Powwow is a diverse tradition, defined by each practitioner and his individual preferences. I have outlined here for you the tradition as I know and practice it. For more information about Powwowing, please visit me online at www.PAGermanPowwow.com.

May God bless you in all that you do.

For further study...

The Long Lost Friend, John George Hohman

Egyptian Secrets of Albertus Magnus

Romanus-buchlein

The Life and Doctrines of Jacob Boehme

The Philosophy of Natural Magic

The Key of Solomon

The Lesser Key of Solomon

A New and Complete Illustration of the Occult Sciences

The Red Church, Chris Bilardi

The Friend in Need, Patrick Donmoyer

God-Given Herbs for the Healing of Mankind, William McGrath

Aspects in Astrology, Sue Tompkins

Made in the USA
Middletown, DE
16 October 2023

40887268R00106